Trick Training Your Bird the Clicker Way

The Click

That Does The Trick

Robin Deutsch

T.F.H. Publications

One TFH Plaza

Third and Union Avenues

Neptune City, NJ 07753

Copyright © 2005 by T.F.H. Publications, Inc.

This book has been published with the intent to provide accurate and authoritative information in regard to the subject matter within. While every precaution has been taken in preparation of this book, the author and publisher expressly disclaim responsibility for any errors, omissions, or adverse effects arising from the use or application of the information contained herein. The techniques and suggestions are used at the reader's discretion and are not to be considered a substitute for veterinary care. If you suspect a medical problem, consult your veterinarian.

Library of Congress Cataloging-in-Publication Data

Deutsch, Robin.

The click that does the trick : trick training your bird the clicker way / Robin Deutsch.

p. cm.

Includes index.

ISBN 0-7938-0561-9 (alk. paper)

1. Cage birds-Training. 2. Cage birds-Behavior. 3. Clicker training (Animal training) I. Title.

SF461.65.D48 2004

636.6'8--dc22

2004018514

Front cover photos by Creatas and Evan Cohen

Back cover photos by Robin Deutsch and John Tyson

Book design by Mary Ann Kahn

www.tfhpublications.com

Contents

The Click That Does The Trick

Understanding Your Bird

Congratulations on your decision to clicker train your bird! Training your bird to perform behaviors or tricks by using a clicker is fun for both you and your pet and it provides more benefits than most people think. Not only does training provide fun and entertainment for your bird and the lucky individuals who get to witness his antics, but it is also is very healthy for his mind.

Birds are extremely intelligent animals, and clicker training your bird will keep his mind occupied, since you're giving him a job to do. This will keep him from becoming depressed or from carrying out self-mutilating behaviors triggered by boredom, such as feather plucking. Most importantly, as you clicker train your bird, you will develop a stronger relationship with him, and the two of you will learn to truly trust one another as you work together. There are only positive outcomes when it comes to clicker training.

Understanding Your Bird's Behaviors

Truly taking the time to understand your bird is one of the keys to successful clicker training. To better understand your bird's behavior, you need to know as much as you can about animal behavior in general and wild birds in particular.

Remember that your parrot is not a fully domesticated animal, and his natural instincts will determine his reactions to new situations.

One of the most important things to keep in mind is that your bird is not a fully domesticated animal like a cat or dog. Even though your bird may have been bred in captivity and be accustomed to a domestic environment, captive-bred birds are still not the same as domesticated animals.

The Power of Natural Instincts

Birds are exotic animals with their natural instincts still intact. Birds rely on those instincts when faced with danger (real or imagined) or an unfamiliar situation. Those instincts dictate their reactions.

For example, have you ever noticed your bird's reaction to a shadow overhead? In the wild, this shadow overhead could be a predator. Therefore, your bird may be wary of the clicker at first or hesitant to perform the behaviors you are trying to teach him. Do not be alarmed—this is perfectly normal. Your bird is simply relying on his instincts.

This is why clicker training birds is somewhat different from using the clicker when training dogs or cats. It is similar in that you are using the same techniques, such as the clicker and the reward, but the difference lies in how the bird views the props. Dogs and cats generally do not have to be introduced to new objects. With birds, you may have to introduce the clicker slowly. Remember, the bird may view this new object as a threat. When you begin to teach a new trick or behavior, the first session usually consists of just getting the bird used to the prop.

If your bird shows any signs of stress or fear, discontinue the training session and give him some affection.

Never push your bird into doing something he is afraid of. This will destroy any trust you build up and will cause him much unneeded stress. Stress can cause not only emotional problems but physical ones as well. If your bird is frightened of the prop and you keep pushing him to use it, he will become even more afraid of it. Let your bird become used to the prop on his own schedule, not yours. This way, when you begin the actual training, it will be more enjoyable for both you and your bird.

Fortunately, birds are also curious by nature. If they see you playing with the object, they may start to play with it, too. Sometimes just leaving the object in sight and near their cages helps them overcome their fear.

Is Playing Basketball Actually Natural?

The majority of the tricks you will teach your bird are actually natural behaviors that you are getting on cue. Never heard of a parrot basketball team in the wild? Well, break down what the basketball trick actually is. Basketball is actually a retrieval behavior. In the wild, it's normal for a bird to bring an object from one place to another. The difference here is that you are having him bring a ball to the hoop.

The scooter trick is an excellent trick for African greys because it appeals to one of their natural instincts. African greys have a natural behavior that looks a lot like chicken scratching. They enjoy going down to the bottoms of their cages and scratching one foot back and forth, which is the same motion needed for the scooter.

Individuality

Even though almost all birds rely on their instincts, you also have to consider your bird's own personality as a factor in training. Every bird is an individual with his own personality and will react differently to different stimuli, and every bird has different preferences regarding behaviors he is willing to learn. Work with your bird at his ability level and attention span.

Although this book was written with the novice bird owner in mind, the instructions provided in this book still apply to those who have owned birds for many years. No matter what your bird's age, what stage of training he's at, or what happened in his past, you will be able to use the clicker as an aid in training.

Think Like a Bird

To predict how your bird will react to any given situation, try to put yourself in his place. Remember that your bird is an intelligent, alert, thinking creature. He doesn't always understand your language or know why you want him to do something. Be patient and calm when your bird reacts strangely.

A Training Game for You

A great way to truly understand what it feels like to be a bird being trained is to play a sort of training game where you become the trainee and get to see what it feels like to be trained. Communication between bird and trainer is mostly non-verbal, and this game puts you in your bird's place.

All you need is a group of friends who are willing to be "bird" trainers. Before you play this game, choose your friends carefully. You are about to become a bird. Because you are the bird and your friends are the trainers, communication between you is limited to using a clicker, whistling, or clapping. It is best not to complicate the game by using gestural cues.

Leave the room while your friends decide on a behavior for you to perform. This could be something very simple, such as sitting down, or it could be a complicated behavior that requires many steps. This is when you find out who your friends really are.

In nature, parrots pick up and carry objects as part of their normal behavior. Carrying a ball to a hoop is not much different.

When you come into the room, you must figure out what the behavior is and whether it's over, which is extremely frustrating because you cannot talk or gesture.

The bird trainers will reward you for correct behavior, and they may have to reward several steps in order to get you to accomplish it.

You might want to quit after a few minutes of total confusion and not knowing what to do. This is how your bird feels! This is why it's necessary to break training down into baby steps, and also why it's important for the bird to feel successful after each session.

Imagine your bird feeling like you do now, not knowing what the trainer wants. As intelligent as a bird is, training will still take time. You must learn how to communicate with your bird. Enjoy this game any time you want to. Get your family and friends into it; it will help them understand what you're doing with your bird.

Successful clicker training is fun for everyone if you always keep in mind that your bird's instincts dictate his actions. Take the time to truly understand your bird, and have fun clicker training him!

9

Dedication

To Chuck Rowles, who taught us. To all the bird trainers around the world, thanks for the wonderful job you do to entertain us all. As always, to my family: Steve, Marcy, and Scott. Finally, to all my birds for making my job fun and easy.

Chapter 1

How to Use
the Clicker
in Training

Clicker training is a method of training based on positive reinforcement. Punishment of any kind is *never* included in clicker training. What is positive reinforcement? Basically, positive reinforcement is using some type of reward during or immediately after a behavior in order to increase the chances of that behavior happening again. For example, if you tell your bird, "Step up," and you give your bird a sunflower seed when he steps up onto your hand or immediately after he steps up, he will be more likely to step up onto your hand the next time you tell him to do so, since he will anticipate the reward.

So where does the clicker fit in? The reward is still used as the bird's motivation for performing the behavior, but if you use the clicker immediately when he performs the desired behavior, you are indicating that the behavior your bird performed was correct. In other words, you are using a clicker to make a connection between a correct behavior and the reward given for performing the behavior correctly. When the clicker is used each and every time the bird does what you want correctly, it acts as a *bridging stimulus*, letting the bird know that he has performed the behavior or trick correctly.

Birds, no matter how intelligent they are, cannot understand exactly what you want them to do. They want to please you, but if they don't understand what you want, it can become very frustrating for all of those involved. The clicker is just one way to let the bird know that what he has done is what you want.

Never tease the bird with the clicker sound—it will confuse your bird, and he will not learn to trust you. If you have young children, they may want to play with the clicker, sounding it on and off. This will also confuse the bird, so keep the clicker out of the hands of children. If the clicker does sound, even if it is by accident, make sure you give the bird a reward.

By using the clicker, trick training becomes easier over time. The bird understands that the clicker means something, and he will understand whether what he has done is correct or not.

Basic Elements of Clicker Training

The Clicker as a Bridging Stimulus

A bridging stimulus is a way of communicating nonverbally that your bird did something correctly. When he hears the familiar clicking sound, he connects his behavior with receiving something positive, a reward. This translates to: "I performed this behavior correctly!" The clicking sound marks the behavior as correct, and the bird will understand that good things come from performing behaviors and tricks correctly.

The clicker tells your bird he is doing the right thing.

When to Use the Clicker

For example: You want the bird to perform the wave. You start off with the bird on the perch. If he shifts his weight, you sound the clicker and reward him. Then, after he understands this, you wait until he performs the next step in the behavior. Perhaps he may lift his foot slightly. You sound the clicker and reward him. Then you wait again. You may have to touch his foot and he may lift it. When he lifts his foot, reward him with the sound of the clicker and the treat. Continue until he does this without needing to be prompted.

It is also possible to use another noise or word as the "bridge." If you decide to use a word as your bridge, make it one word that you don't normally use all the time. The bird must associate the word or noise with performing a behavior correctly and with receiving a reward. The clicker, however, seems to be the bridge that is easiest for birds—and most other pets—to understand.

Cues

To teach any behavior or trick, you need to use some type of cue. A cue is simply a signal that will indicate the specific behavior you would like your bird to perform; it is used to elicit a desired response. A cue may be verbal (words, sounds), nonverbal (gestures, hand signals), or environmental (sights, smells).

Gestural cues can be any gesture or hand signal, and they do not have to be very pronounced or exaggerated once your bird has learned the cues—they can be so subtle that they are unnoticeable to anyone watching. A verbal cue should be as short and simple as possible, two words at the most.

Environmental cues are simply any type of cues your bird will pick up on easily. For instance, when a bird sees an object such as a bell in front of him and goes over to ring it, he has responded to an environmental cue.

Any of these cues can be used alone or paired with other cue types. For instance, you place a basketball hoop and ball on the table in front of your bird (environmental cue). You then point to the ball (nonverbal cue) and say, "Play ball" (verbal cue). You follow that by pointing to the hoop (nonverbal cue).

Parrots can learn to recognize verbal, gestural, and environmental cues.

When first teaching a trick, you may need to exaggerate your cues. After your bird has learned the behavior, you can "fade" the cues slowly. Eventually you may be able to use just a non-verbal cue to get your bird to perform most behaviors.

You probably have already taught your bird to respond to some cues without realizing it. If your bird steps up onto your hand when you hold it out to him, he is responding to a gestural cue. If you prompt him with the words "Up" or "Step up," he is responding to a verbal cue.

Cues—and any training—can work both ways. Your bird may have actually trained you with his own cues. If you run over to your bird when he screams, he has taught you to respond to his cue. If you are not teaching your bird, your bird will teach you. This is why many people have "problem" birds; they did not realize what they were teaching their birds to do.

Positive Reinforcers

Positive reinforcers are rewards used to ensure the repetition of a desired behavior, and they are powerful tools when used to influence behavior. Reinforcers may be primary (food) or secondary (social reward). A positive reinforcer that works with one bird will not necessarily work with another. You need to know your bird well enough to choose a reinforcer that your bird likes and will respond to.

Social reinforcement is the easiest reward to use. You can always give your bird a cuddle or kiss without having to go to the kitchen to get it. Social rewards also help you establish a nurturing bond. It is vital that you establish a good and loving relationship with your bird, and the social rewards and the trust you will develop while clicker training will help establish a good relationship with him right from the start.

Overall, birds just seem to work harder for secondary reinforcers. They love affection and will do almost anything to get it. A cuddle, a scratch on the head, and the applause of an appreciative audience are all excellent secondary reinforcers. It's best to think of your bird as a companion first and a performer second.

Use small food rewards—not handfuls of seed—when training your bird. If the reward is too big, he will become full and less interested in further rewards.

Primary reinforcers should be included in training, however, and they must be small enough that your bird does not spend more time eating than he does learning the behavior that you are trying to teach him. In other words, don't give him a whole nut each time you reward him. Instead, give him a small portion. This also keeps his attention on the behavior.

Food Rewards to Use as Reinforcers

When deciding on which foods to use as rewards, make sure to choose a favorite food item that can be given in very small pieces. This item should not be part of the bird's regular diet.

Pistachios, pine nuts, and sunflower seeds are often used for birds. Don't use whole nuts or large seeds as rewards. A small piece of food will encourage him without allowing him to gorge himself. The treats must be small enough so the bird can eat it quickly but large enough that the bird will be willing to work for it. I cut peanuts or pistachio nuts into quarters, and I find that works very well for medium to large birds. For smaller birds, I use either a sunflower seed or millet. Some birds will not want a treat but will ask for affection instead.

It is absolutely *not* recommended to place your bird on any kind of restrictive training diet. This is best left to professional animal trainers. An improper training diet can harm your bird.

Introducing the Clicker

Step 1

Go over to your bird's cage with the clicker in one of your hands and the treat in the other. Sound the clicker and then immediately reward your bird with a treat. It is very important that the reward is immediate. If you wait too long to give the reward, the effectiveness of the clicker is gone.

At first, the clicker may startle your bird, but if you remain calm and reassuring, the bird will get over his nervousness. A nervous bird or one who startles more easily may take several days to get used to the clicker.

Some birds may also do better if they can touch and play with the clicker at first. In the very beginning this is acceptable, but once your bird understands what the clicker is for, you should no longer allow him to play with it. Birds are very curious, and letting them handle the clicker may help them get over any fears they may have. The clicker is not loud, but some birds need more time. When you introduce the clicker patiently, you allow your bird to learn to trust both you and the clicker. Remember, one of the most important keys to training is trust.

Once your bird seems comfortable with the clicker—not scared or disturbed by its presence—move on to step 2.

Step 2

After a day or so of doing this, the bird will start to associate the clicker with receiving the reward. Now instead of just giving the bird a treat for doing nothing, reach out with your finger as if you are going to pick him up. When he moves his foot even slightly, sound the clicker and reward him immediately. The idea behind this step is to teach the bird that he has to do something and not just sit there to get the reward.

You don't have to use this trick; you can use any trick. This is just an easy example for getting your bird to understand that he has to perform a behavior in order to receive the reward.

The bird should start to understand that he has to do something to get the

For effective training, reward your bird immediately after he performs the desired behavior.

clicker sound and the reward. Once your bird understands this concept, you can now move on to clicker training your bird to perform tricks and other behaviors!

The first trick you teach may take your bird longer to learn just because he is getting used to and understanding what the clicker does. As time goes on, your bird will learn behaviors faster because he knows what the clicker means.

Chapter 2

Essential
Training
Guidelines

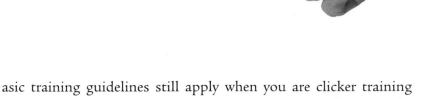

Basic training guidelines still apply when you are clicker training your bird. These guidelines are just as important to follow as the instructions involved with using the clicker.

Only have one person as the primary trainer. Once the bird has learned a behavior, then others can work with him. Make sure that they work exactly the same way as you have. It is helpful to record how you train your bird.

Chaining Small Steps Together

Before you attempt to train your bird, think carefully about the behavior. If it is a complicated one, break it down into smaller steps. Each step is taught in sequence before moving onto the next one. This is called *chaining*. If you break the behavior down into several steps, each part will be easier to learn. You can then chain all of the steps of the behavior together once your bird has mastered each one of them.

Obviously this will require you to plan ahead. You may not realize how many individual actions go into even the simplest behavior. For instance, to shake

To train any bird, you need a relationship that has a good foundation in trust.

someone's hand requires that you lift and extend your right hand in a horizontal position toward someone else, grasp his or her hand in yours, squeeze gently but firmly, and shake it up and down. Then you must let go.

Sometimes it's a good idea to write down each step. If you are unsure what you want your bird to do, he will be even more lost, so by writing down the steps, you clearly outline what you would like your bird to do and will be able to relay these steps to your bird. As your bird learns one step, move on to the next one.

Break down each behavior into steps and train each step in sequence. The first step in answering the phone is for your bird to approach the phone.

Making Training Fun

Training sessions should be fun and enjoyable for both you and your bird. Make these sessions something you look forward to, and don't make them too long. Your bird's attention span will dictate how long they should be, but end before the fun is gone.

You do not want training to be more stressful than it absolutely has to be. If your bird is afraid or unhappy, he will not enjoy training sessions. This can lead to unacceptable levels of stress.

Top Ten Essential Training Guidelines

1. Never work a bird who is sick or shows any signs of stress.

2. If you or your bird show any signs of frustration, back up a step or end the training session on a positive note by switching to another behavior the bird already knows. You can then rethink the situation or behavior to determine how to avoid further problems.

3. Be consistent. Do not change a behavior once you start. Do not confuse the bird.

4. Never work with the bird if you are angry or upset. It should be fun for both of you.

5. Try working in a quiet area without any distractions (training is not a spectator sport), and learn to judge your bird's attention span.

6. Only work on one behavior at a time. Wait until the bird has learned one behavior before going onto the next.

7. Reinforce a desired behavior immediately every time it occurs until it has been learned. This increases the likelihood that it will occur again.

8. Determine what your bird considers to be a reward. This could be a favorite food item or affection. If you use food as a reward, pair it with affection so that you can gradually phase out the food and still reward the behavior. Rewards should be easy to give, and they should not disturb the training session. If this is a food treat, use a small piece each time.

9. Keep verbal commands short and easy to remember.

10. Always end on a positive note. You want the bird to enjoy the training sessions as much as you do. Remember, your bird wants to please you. He just might not understand what you want him to do.

Always end your sessions on a positive note. If your bird seems frustrated or upset with a particular behavior, switch to another one that he already knows. Reward him for this behavior and end the session. Take a break and analyze what went wrong. You may have been giving your bird unclear cues or trying to teach too much at one time.

Environment

Always be aware of the things that are happening around you. If your bird reacts negatively to a situation, try to determine the cause. Think carefully about what happened before, during, and after the incident. Your bird may react to a perceived threat that you didn't notice.

Be prepared for the unusual. Birds often react to overhead objects or shadows as dangers, while we take these things for granted. For example, to a bird, an electrical cord may resemble a snake, and a moving shadow could be mistaken for a predator, such as a hawk or monkey.

Furthermore, even though showing your bird off to friends and family is something we all like to do, don't expect your bird to perform well in strange surroundings with lots of strange people around, especially if small, excitable children are jumping and running close by.

If your bird is distracted—for example, by his cage mate—the training session will be ineffective.

Make sure to train in an area without distractions. Birds don't always have much of an attention span as it is, and anything that can distract them, will.

Close supervision is necessary when allowing others to handle your bird.

Things such as kids running around, a TV blasting away, phones ringing, etc., are always so much more interesting than having to work.

Training Schedule

Try to develop some kind of schedule, and make training time a set time. This does not mean that training starts at precisely 7 p.m. You can train around that time, sometimes a little before or a little later; just make it regular. Once your bird has learned the behavior, you can start to work with him at different times in front of a small group, like your family.

Don't Train Negative Behaviors

Many people unknowingly reinforce their bird's negative behaviors. When a bird screams, many owners rush over to the cage, gesturing and screaming at the bird to shut up. These owners do not realize that they have just trained their bird to exhibit a negative behavior.

As is true with children, birds perceive negative attention as better than no attention at all. A bored or lonely bird may actually enjoy the little show that his human puts on every time he screams. Screaming fulfills many functions for a bird in the wild: They

Keep in mind that a little time and patience can work wonders!

scream to alert the flock to dangers; they scream to maintain contact with other flock members or mates; they scream as part of territorial defense; sometimes they scream just for enjoyment.

Be Creative

Each bird adjusts differently. Learn how to gauge your bird's attention span, his desire to learn and to work, and, most importantly, the enjoyment that he gets out of training.

Remember that the extent of your bird's training is limited only by your own imagination. Go to toy stores and check out the infant and toddler section.

Each bird is an individual. Tailor your training sessions to your bird's unique needs and preferences.

Maybe your bird is a budding Einstein and would like simple shape puzzles. Maybe your bird is more musically inclined. Many larger birds can learn to shake a tambourine or hit it against a perch.

If you're handy, you can even build many different kinds of props. In the back of this book are instructions on how to create the props used in the tricks described. However, you can also come up with your own ideas for props and tricks, but keep your bird's safety in mind at all times. Make sure any props you buy or make are safe. Always remember, if your bird shows any signs of frustration, back up a step or two.

The important thing to remember is that both you and your bird have fun. At my house, whenever we have a training session, all my birds want to go first. They hate when the sessions end. So good luck, and may you and your future star have fun.

Chapter 3

Training
Natural Behaviors
on Command

Once your bird is comfortable with the clicker and both of you understand the basic concepts of clicker training, you can start teaching your bird tricks and behaviors on cue. It's best to start at a beginner's level, using the clicker to train natural behaviors, which are behaviors that a bird does instinctively. These are easy to train because all you need to do is to catch the bird when he is doing them naturally and then use the clicker and reward to show him that this is a correct behavior. You can easily train your bird to do any of the behaviors in this chapter, and you can even encourage other behaviors that you see your bird doing on his own.

The Nod

Any size bird can learn to do the nod because most birds already nod on their own. Some birds bob their heads when excited, while others use the nod when talking or making noise. The trick is to get them to do this on cue.

Whenever you see your bird bobbing his head, sound the clicker and immediately reward your bird. Again, this works best if the bird understands the meaning of the clicker. It may take longer to train if he does not.

Nodding is a natural behavior and therefore an easy trick to train your bird to perform.

Another method is to show the bird a treat, moving it up and down. Your bird will follow the treat. When he does so, click and then reward him.

Before you start any training, decide what cue you are going to use. This cue could be verbal and/or gestural. A little word of advice, however: make the actual cue something a little bit more imaginative than moving your fingers up and down. Most people move their fingers in an upward or downward motion when looking at a bird, and this will inadvertently signal his cue for the nod. He will soon become very frustrated because he is doing what he is asked but is not receiving a reward for it. Therefore, use a different verbal or gestural cue when teaching the nod.

The Head Shake "No"

This is another behavior that all birds do naturally. Birds normally shake their heads after preening, playing, and other normal activities. Try to reward your bird by using the clicker and a treat immediately after you see your bird doing this.

If your bird does not frequently shake his head naturally, you can try to blow gently in his face. *Gentle* is the key word in this situation: don't scare your bird or knock him over. When you do this, a bird's natural response is to shake his head. When he shakes his head, sound the clicker and reward him.

As with all training, make the real cue something that is not obvious to others. It will impress your friends more if they don't see a hand cue or signal.

Always use the cue at the start of any training and stay with it throughout.

By training your bird to perform his natural swaying behavior on command, you can make it appear that he is dancing.

The Dance

Many large birds will sway or rock back and forth when they want something. This is a begging motion that can easily be turned into a dance.

Decide on a cue before you even start to train any behavior. These cues can be exaggerated at first and then slowly diminished until no one but you and your bird actually notice the cue.

When you see your bird starting to rock back and forth, rock back and forth with him, using that as his cue to dance. Reward him for doing so, either with a treat reward or with affection. Every time you see your bird rock back and forth, cue the behavior, click, and then reward. Soon your bird will respond to the cue without having initiated the behavior. When this happens, sound the clicker and reward.

Once he is comfortable doing the behavior, diminish the cue until it's something as small as a finger moving slightly from side to side. This is a behavior that most of the bigger birds can do because lifting their feet is a

Waving is just a modification of the motions your bird uses to step up on your hand.

natural behavior for them. Even smaller birds can learn this behavior, though it might be difficult to get them to do the sway/dance initially.

The Wave

Begin this behavior with your bird placed on a T-stand, and go over to your bird as if you were going to pick him up.

When your bird lifts his foot to step up on your hand, sound your clicker and use the command "Wave" and/or a hand cue if you so desire. Give the reward. Repeat, always using the command "Wave"—and the hand cue, if you are using one—and never the command "Up" when teaching this behavior. Soon your bird will lift up his foot on his own without trying to step onto your hand and will appear to be waving at you. Sometimes just tapping him gently on the foot will get him to raise it up high. To get him to raise it up higher, you can lift your finger to the point where you want him to lift his foot.

Reward and praise even the smallest motion at first.

The Wing Flap

Another natural behavior for birds is flapping their wings. This can easily be turned into a cued trick, one that you can teach in several ways.

Method One

Hold your cueing hand with your index and little fingers extended and your thumb, middle, and ring fingers folded, forming a U. With the bird on your other hand, move your cueing hand toward his wings. Cue your bird verbally, saying, "Wings." You may need to actually touch his wings with your index and little fingers at first. Usually a slight pressure on the front of

Flapping on command is another easy trick that any bird can learn. Teaching your bird to perform natural behaviors when cued lays the groundwork for training more complex tricks.

his folded wings will cause him to pull back and flap. Remember that even though you have touched the wings with your fingers, it was the start of the hand cue that you will be using. When your bird successfully flaps his wings (even if you had to help him do so), click and reward immediately.

This cue takes a lot of practice. As your bird learns to respond to the verbal and hand cue, slowly fade out the hand cue. Instead of touching your bird's wings each time, only hold the hand cue close to the bird. Gradually move your cueing hand farther away.

Method Two
Hold the bird on one hand. Tilt your hand slightly backward, causing the bird to flap his wings to regain his balance. Use the verbal cue "Wings" each time. You can use the hand cue described in the first method if you wish. When he performs this successfully, sound the clicker and then reward. This method works very well with smaller birds.

Method Three: The "Eagle" Method
This is a variation on the Wings trick. However, instead of flapping his wings, your bird will hold them outstretched, imitating an eagle. With the

Playing peek-a-boo is a cute and endearing trick to teach your bird. It is sure to entertain your family and friends.

bird perched on your hand, slowly raise it to eye level. Give the command "Eagle" and either rotate your hand very slightly backward or drop it very slightly (1-2 inches). Click and reward when he does this.

Peek-A-Boo

A variation on the Wings or Eagle behavior is peek-a-boo. When preening or stretching, many species of birds will stretch one wing to bring it closer to their face. Whenever this happens, sound the clicker and reward with affection or a treat. Say "Peek-a-boo" each time. You can also physically move your bird's wing to cover his eyes, say "Peek-a-boo," sound the clicker, and reward.

Chapter 4

Easy Tricks

Whatever behavior you are training, you must first introduce the prop. This needs to be done slowly, so that the bird feels comfortable and safe around the prop.

Start with the prop on the table at a "safe" distance from the bird. This could be all the way at the other end of the table. Some birds are more timid than others, while some are more inquisitive. If your bird is the timid type, start with the prop farther away. If your bird is the curious sort, you can probably start with the prop closer.

Have your clicker and treat ready. Whenever your bird moves toward the prop, sound the clicker and give the bird the treat immediately. It may take a few minutes to several days before the bird feels safe enough to go close enough to the prop.

Once he is going to the prop, you can move on to step 2.

Always end any session on a positive note.

Tips to Remember

- Remember to reward each small step and to use plenty of praise.
- If the bird seems to be confused or is frustrated, go back a step or two and do something that he knows.
- End any session on a positive note.

Turnaround

Level	Easy
Equipment	Stand, treats
Type of Bird	Any bird
Training Sessions	2-15 minutes
Training Objective	The bird will completely turn around on cue.
Trick Analysis	The turnaround is one of the easier behaviors to teach any bird. It is a natural behavior because it is one that birds do all the time, without any prompting. You can teach this behavior to any bird from budgie to macaw.

Step 1

Place the bird on the stand, then hold the treat off to one side. Your bird will need to turn his head to get the treat. Click and reward the bird with plenty of praise and cuddles.

Step 2

Repeat step 1 several times until the bird understands that by turning his head, he gets the reward. At this point in the behavior, start using the turnaround cue. One cue is to hold your index finger pointing out and down and make a circular motion with it. You may also choose to use another cue, perhaps by saying, "Turn around."

Step 3

Move the treat slightly farther behind the bird's head. He will find it harder to reach for the treat without moving his body—he'll have to turn at least a slight distance to get the treat. When he does, sound the clicker and reward him with the treat and praise.

When he does this movement easily, start moving the treat behind him. To get it, he will need to turn around completely. Remember to show him the treat, moving it around to the back of him as you do so.

Step 4

You will probably need to use both hands for this step. Give the cue, show the treat, and move it behind the bird. Then, using your other hand, move it to the other side so that your bird will need to turn his head to retrieve the goody.

After this is done and he understands that he'll have to turn even more to receive the reward, complete the turnaround by showing him the treat behind him and then switching hands, moving the treat around to the front. The bird should be making a complete turnaround now. You may need to do this in two steps to begin with, stopping when the bird turns halfway around and then completing the turnaround after this pause. Eventually eliminate the treat at the halfway point and have your bird complete the turnaround.

Remember that plenty of praise, cuddles, and enthusiasm work wonders.

Somersault

Level	Easy
Equipment	Stand, treats
Type of Bird	Most birds
Training Session	2-15 minutes per session
Training Objective	Bird will complete a full somersault.
Trick Analysis	The somersault requires a lot of patience in training but is easy for birds who often perform antics that seem acrobatic (many birds do!). Some birds are not very acrobatic and may not be able to do this behavior. Watch your bird at play. If you see your bird has acrobatic displays, then he's ready to perform the somersault.

Step 1

Place your bird on a stand and then move the treat below him; he will need to move his head down to retrieve the treat. Do this several times, using the clicker when he moves his head down and rewarding with not only the treat but also with plenty of praise and affection.

Step 2

Come up with a visual cue. One visual cue could be pointing your index finger at a horizontal angle and making a circular motion, along with using the verbal cue "Somersault." Start using this cue with the behavior.

Step 3

Begin this step once the bird feels comfortable bending down to get the treat. You will need to use your other hand for this next part. Move the treat down as in the first step; then, using your other hand, move it lower and slightly behind the bird. The bird will need to almost hang upside down. Click and reward.

Step 4

Move your hand with the treat so the bird has to go down and over the perch to get it. This is a more difficult step for many birds. It will also take longer to achieve this goal than did the previous steps. Be patient, and if your bird shows any sign of frustration or fear, back up and don't push. Sound the clicker and reward your bird for whatever he can do. If he does the somersault, click and reward with lots of praise and affection—clap and show enthusiasm for what he just did.

Hamster Wheel

Difficulty Level	Easy
Equipment Needed	Hamster wheel (can be bought at any pet store)
Type of Bird	Small birds, such as budgies
Training Session	Only a few minutes per session; otherwise you might stress the bird.
Trick Objective	Bird will jog in the hamster wheel.
Trick Analysis	In the beginning, you might want to have the opening facing your body instead of

facing away from your body. It will give the bird a more secure feeling to know that you are close by.

This behavior is geared toward little birds, unlike most behaviors, which are suited for large birds.

Step 1

Figure out a cue and use it each time. This is a very easy behavior to train little birds to perform. Some budgies actually love hamster wheels as toys in their cages. As with every behavior, the first step is to get the bird used to the prop. Once he is use to the prop, go on to step 2.

Step 2

Place the bird inside the prop. Click, reward, and praise your bird for being inside the wheel. Once the bird is comfortable with staying inside the wheel, go on to step 3.

Step 3

Move the wheel slightly so the bird has to walk forward. Sound the clicker, reward, and praise. Go on to step 4 when the bird is doing this each time.

Step 4

Place the bird inside the wheel and wait. See if he starts to walk on his own. If not, move the wheel again so he has to walk. Once he is walking a few steps on his own, go to step 5. Remember to use the clicker, reward, and praise each time.

Step 5

The bird should now know that he has to walk to move the wheel to get his reward. Hold off until he walks several times. Eventually he will walk or jog in the wheel.

Alternative method

If you have an especially lazy bird, you can train him to hold onto the wheel while you spin it. Do not spin it too fast or you may injure the bird. In this case, your bird must be comfortable with sitting in the wheel and with the wheel moving.

Hamster Ball

Difficulty Level	Easy
Equipment Needed	Hamster ball/guinea pig ball
Type of Bird	Any size bird that will fit into the appropriately sized ball
Training Session	10-15 minutes per session
Trick Objective	The bird will go inside the ball and run.

Step 1

Figure out a cue and use it each time. Allow the bird to get used to the prop. Offer praise and rewards. Once the bird is comfortable around the ball, go on to step 2.

It's best not to put the ball on a table, because your bird could easily fall off and become injured. If you put the bird in the ball on the floor, be sure that he does not crash into objects and that other pets can't hurt him.

Introduce your bird to the hamster ball slowly. Many birds are afraid of such enclosed spaces at first.

Step 2

Place the bird's favorite treat inside the hamster ball. Make sure it is stable so it does not roll around. Use the clicker, reward, and praise. When the bird is comfortable inside the ball, go on to step 3.

Step 3

Put the lid on the ball very carefully, making sure you do not get tail, feathers, or feet inside the lid. Wait a few seconds, praising and talking to your bird while he is inside the ball. Open the lid, clicker, reward, and praise. When you can stretch this out, go on to step 4.

Be careful not to catch your bird's feet or tail in the lid. That will make him afraid of the ball.

Once he is in the ball, start rewarding your bird only when he walks. Gradually lengthen the distance he must travel.

Step 4

Place the ball down on a very smooth surface. Rugs or ceramic tiles on the floor may make it harder for your bird to move the ball. Give the ball a very gentle push so that the bird has to walk. Do not push too hard or you may injure the bird.

Remember, your bird should go slow and easy so that he enjoys the training as much as you do. If you go slowly, the bird will trust you more. Once he is walking a few steps on his own, go on to step 5. Remember to use the clicker, reward, and praise.

Step 5

The bird should be taking a few steps inside the ball. Now you need to draw it out. Instead of rewarding every few steps, wait until he is moving farther. With each step, allow the bird to go farther.

If you want, you can put the ball on a track. If you have more than one bird, you can have races.

Go-Cart

Difficulty Level	Easy
Equipment Needed	Hamster go-cart
Type of Bird	Small birds (such as cockatiels)
Training Session	10-15 minutes per session
Trick Objective	The bird will go inside the go-cart and start to run or jog.

Step 1

Figure out a cue. This behavior is taught the same way as the hamster ball behavior; the only exception is that it does not roll all over—instead, it rolls straight. Allow your bird to get used to the prop by offering praise and rewards.

Step 2

Place the bird's favorite treat inside the go-cart wheel. Make sure it is stable so that it does not roll forward or backward. Use the clicker, reward, and praise. When the bird is comfortable inside the go-cart wheel, go on to step 3.

Step 3

Put the lid on the go-cart wheel very carefully, making sure you do not get tail, feathers, or feet inside the lid. The space inside the wheel is smaller than the space inside the ball, so the bird may have a harder time with this step.

If your pet store doesn't carry hamster go-carts, they might special order one for you, or you can search for one on the Internet.

Wait a few seconds, praising and talking to the bird while he is inside the go-cart wheel. Open the lid, clicker, reward, and praise. When you can stretch this out, go on to step 4.

Step 4

Place the wheel inside the go-cart and put it down on a very smooth surface. Rugs or ceramic tiles on the floor may make it harder for the bird to move the go-cart. Give the go-cart a very gentle push so that the bird has to walk. Do not push too hard, or else you may injure your bird.

The first step of training any trick is to allow the bird to get used to the prop.

Remember, you want the bird to go slow and easy, so that he enjoys the training as much as you do. If you go slowly, your bird will trust you more.

Step 5

The bird should be taking a few steps inside the go-cart. Now you need to draw it out. Instead of rewarding every few steps, wait until he is moving farther. With each step, allow the bird to go farther.

Once your bird is walking a few steps in the cart, keep increasing the distance he has to go for his reward until you reach the distance you want him to go.

Ladder Climb

Difficulty Level	Easy
Equipment Needed	Ladder
Type of Bird	Any, but it may be hard to find a big enough ladder for larger birds. (An inexpensive one can be made from dowels.)
Training Session	10-15 minutes per session. It will depend on the bird's attention level.
Trick Objective	The bird will walk up the ladder.
Trick Analysis	The ladder will be placed on the floor or table, and the bird will walk up it.

The ladder behavior can be performed in many ways. Small birds seem to love ladders, and they can easily be trained to go up and down. If you start with your bird on the floor and offer him the ladder, he will most likely start walking upward. This is because most birds do not like being on the floor.

Most small birds will climb ladders readily, so this trick is especially easy to teach.

Step 1

Don't forget to figure out a cue and to allow the bird to get used to the prop. Most birds already have a ladder in their cages and are used to going up and down. If they are, you can add some additional steps.

Step 2

Placing a treat toward the top of the ladder, allow the bird to step up onto the first rung. When he does, sound the clicker, reward, and praise. When he does that each time, go on to step 3.

Step 3

Hold off on the treat until your bird

walks up several rungs of the ladder, then click, reward, and praise. When he does this easily, go on to step 4.

Step 4

Withhold the treat until the bird walks up all the rungs of the ladder. Sound the clicker, reward, and praise. You may end it here or go on to step 5.

Step 5

In this extension of the ladder trick, your bird will walk across a rope or perch that is attached to the ladder. The other side will also have a ladder attached. Offer the treat, allowing the bird to take a few steps on the perch. When he does this each time, go on to step 6. Use the clicker, reward, and praise each time.

For larger birds, instead of walking across a rope or perch to the other side, you can have them slide down a post.

Step 6

When the bird goes across the perch to the other side, use the treat to get the bird to step back onto the ladder. When he does, click, reward, and praise. When this happens consistently, go onto step 7.

Once your bird is climbing the ladder reliably, you can start having him walk across a perch or tightrope.

Step 7

Your bird will go up one side and across the perch to the other ladder. Don't give him his reward yet; instead, hold off. Place the treat on the table so he has to go down the ladder to get the treat. Sound the clicker, reward, and praise.

Eventually, the bird will go up one side, across the perch, and then down the other side.

Step 8—Optional

You can also train the bird to pick up a little barbell to use for balancing, go across the "tightrope," put the barbell down, and then go down the ladder.

Rocking Horse

Difficulty Level	Easy
Equipment Needed	Rocking horse with a perch attached
Type of Bird	Any size bird, but you need to fit the size of the rocking horse to the size of the bird.
Training Session	10-20 minutes per session. However, if your bird enjoys riding around on the horse, you can extend the session.
Trick Objective	To get the bird to ride on the horse and rock back and forth.
Trick Analysis	The bird can be put onto the horse or walk over to the horse and climb on. The bird will then allow the trainer to either rock the horse, or the bird can cause the horse to rock.

Step 1

Pick a cue you want to use. Start with getting the bird used to the prop. Use the clicker, reward, and praise.

Step 2

Once your bird is comfortable being near the prop, you can put him on it. Make sure that it does not fall over or rock. Go slowly. When he sits on the prop, sound the clicker, reward, and praise. Keep doing this, lengthening the amount of time he sits on the prop.

Step 3

Slowly rock the horse for him. Keep offering praise while you do this. Sound the clicker, reward, and praise. Keep doing this until he allows you to rock him back and forth several times. Then go to step 4.

Step 4

Hold the treat in front of him and allow him to reach for it, making sure the prop does not fall over. By reaching for the treat, he will lean his weight forward, rocking the horse. When he does this, sound the clicker, reward, and praise. Keep doing this; then hold off on giving the treat right away. He will need to rock back and forth several times before he gets the reward.

Ring Toss

Level	Easy
Equipment	Peg on a base and rings
Type of Bird	Any species, but props must be adjusted to the bird's size.
Training Time	2-15 minutes per session
Training Objective	The bird will pick up the rings or take them from your hand and place them on a peg.
Trick Analysis	You need to have in mind exactly how you are going to break this behavior down into small steps before you start to train. Keep these goals and your objective in mind prior to training.

Have your verbal and/or hand cue ready to use at the onset of the behavior. As with all behaviors, there are many different ways to go about teaching your bird. Select one that you find works the best for both you and your bird.

Variation 1

Step 1

Introduce the prop. In this case, it works best to have the prop—rings and peg—at one end of the table and your bird at the other. Click and reward when he moves toward the props. Keep at it until he consistently goes over the prop and gets close enough to touch it. Then move on to step 2.

Step 2

Now that your bird is going over to the prop (the rings as well), the next step is to touch the prop with his beak. Try holding off on giving the treat. Wait a few seconds. Some birds will touch the prop in frustration. This is what you want. Sound that clicker and reward immediately.

Keep repeating until he understands that by touching the prop, he will be rewarded. If he doesn't touch the prop, you may need to lure him over with the treat reward. Show him the treat; lay it on top of the prop's stem. When he reaches for it and his beak touches the prop, sound the clicker and reward.

Keep doing this until he consistently takes the treat. After a few sessions, do not put the treat down; just point or tap the stem of the prop. He will touch the prop, hoping that you will put the treat down. Use the clicker and reward the bird.

Once he is doing this with no hesitation, you're ready for step 3.

Step 3

Hold a ring over the stem of the prop near your bird's beak, and when he touches it, click and reward. The touch may be a microsecond long or he may

In Step 3, you will be dropping the ring on the post when your bird touches it. In time, he'll drop it on the post himself.

actually take it in his beak. When he is touching a ring on a regular basis, start extending the amount of time that he's touching it.

Hold off on sounding the clicker. Some birds will get angry or frustrated and grab hold of the ring for a longer time. Sound the clicker and reward.

Continue stretching out the time the bird is holding the rings. When you have accomplished this, move on to step 4. Always end any session on a positive note. If your bird appears too frustrated, go back a step or two and end the session on something he knows.

Step 4

With a ring placed slightly below the top of the stem, have your bird take hold of it. When he does, he should let go. If he does (without pulling the ring off first), the ring should drop onto the stem. Sound the clicker and reward.

Keep doing this until he feels comfortable with it. When he does, start moving the ring higher. Go on to step 5 when he is able to take hold of the rings slightly above the stem and drop them over the stem.

Step 5

Hold the rings above and a little away from the prop. The bird must move closer to get the rings on the stem, so this could take a little time. Remember that all birds learn at different rates. There is nothing wrong with a bird who can't figure out a behavior in a week or two—or a month or two. Relax and enjoy the time with your bird.

After each successful completion of a ring on the peg, start to move the rings farther away. Your bird should walk a few steps over to the prop, put the rings on the peg, and then get the reward. Go slowly and enjoy yourself.

Remember to gear each prop to the right size for the bird. You don't want to have a little parakeet trying to lift a ring for a macaw. It could be little birdie hernia time if you do. Use your common sense. If this way doesn't sound like something you want to use, try the next variation.

Variation 2

Step 1

With the prop on the table, place the bird as close to it as you can without scaring him. This could be at the opposite end of the table at first. Allow him to feel comfortable around the prop. Start moving it closer and closer to him,

As a variation of this trick, you can have your bird remove the rings from the post and bring them to you.

waiting each time to see his reaction. Use that clicker and those treat rewards each time the bird either goes near the prop or allows the prop to be moved closer to him.

Some birds will go right over to the prop, while others tend to shy away from it. There is no need to rush the bird. Training takes time, especially if you want the bird to enjoy it and trust you.

When he feels comfortable around the prop and will let you move the prop right next to him, you are ready for step 2.

Step 2

Once the bird is accustomed to the prop being near him, pick up one of the rings. If he touches it, sound the clicker and give him his special treat.

You could also lure him to a ring placed in front of him on the table by setting the treat on top of the ring. To get the treat, he must touch the ring. Some birds will do this faster than others.

If your bird doesn't respond right away, don't give up. Birds learn at different rates. It does not mean you have a stupid bird. Some birds are naturally curious about things around them and are more likely to pick up and touch objects. Other birds are more shy and timid. By going slowly and being positive, you are building your bird's confidence.

If your bird is touching the rings consistently, you are ready for step 3.

Step 3

The next time that he touches the rings, wait before sounding the clicker. Your bird may take hold of it in frustration; this is what you want him to do. Sound that clicker and reward him.

Increase the amount of time that he holds the ring in his beak. This step may happen right away or it may take several days or a few weeks to accomplish.

When he is doing this, you are ready for step 4.

Step 4

Now that your bird will take hold of the rings for a few seconds, it is time to move your other hand (the one not holding the clicker) close to the bird. When you cue him to pick up the ring,

Training takes time. Enjoy the time you spend with your bird.

move your hand under the ring he just picked up. When he drops the ring, it should drop in your hand. Sound the clicker and reward him.

Keep doing this until he gets the idea that he is supposed to put the ring in your hand. This can take several days or more before he understands.

When he can do this, move on to step 5.

Step 5

Once he is dropping the ring in your hand, you can start moving your hand farther away from him, but closer to the prop. Move your hand only slightly. Each time he can put the ring in your hand, you can move farther away. If he is responding to this, he understands what it is you want. Now you can move your hand directly over the prop. Once again, birds differ in how long it will take to train any given behavior. When they understand the training game, they learn other behaviors faster.

When he has finished this step, you can go on to step 6.

Step 6

With your hand directly over the prop, allow the post to show through your fingers. You don't want any portion of it sticking up yet, just showing. As he repeatedly places the ring in your hand, remember to sound the clicker and to give the reward with each success.

Allow more and more of the post to show through your fingers. Do this until your hand is resting on the bottom of the prop and most of the ring shows.

When he'll give you the ring without hesitation, move on to step 7.

Step 7

Slowly start to phase out your hand. Some birds will figure out that you want the rings on the peg and not in your hand. Other birds will need you to do this very slowly, by backing your hand away by inches at a time, until it is no longer near the prop.

By now the bird is picking up the rings right by the prop and placing them on the peg.

When this is accomplished, you can go to step 8.

Step 8

Your bird is now performing the complete behavior. Move the rings farther and farther away from the peg. Do this until the bird has to pick up the rings and walk several steps before placing the rings on the peg.

If at any time your bird appears frustrated, or just refuses to work, back up a step or two and do something he knows. If he becomes too frustrated, he will not enjoy working. You want this to be enjoyable for both you and your bird.

Always end any session—even one where you had to back up a step or two—on a positive note. You want your bird to feel as if he has succeeded, not failed. He really does want to please you, but he may not understand what it is that you want him to do. Keep working at it in short sessions.

While the first method sounds a lot faster and much simpler, it may not work for every bird. Some birds learn differently than others. By taking more time with a first-time behavior, the other behaviors become easier to teach. Other birds will figure out the training game after only a few minutes. They might be the ones who can pick up a behavior in a few short tries.

Some trainers prefer the second method because it sets up the bird for other behaviors such as basketball, banking, etc. These are all forms of retrieval behaviors.

I prefer the first method. Train using whichever method you like best; just remember to use those clickers and rewards, and end each session on a positive note.

Variation 3

Removing the Rings

If you have more than one bird and have trained other retrieval behaviors besides this one, you can have one bird put the rings on and another remove them. This is why knowing the basic retrieval will help a bird learn other variations.

Show the bird the rings that are on the peg. When he touches them, reward him. Lift each ring even with the post so he doesn't have to work very hard to get them off and into your hand.

Each time he understands a step, go on to the next. Lower the ring on the peg until, finally, he takes them off completely and puts them in your hand or on the table.

Variation 4

The Patriotic Parrot

Parrots can see colors and distinguish between them. Because of this ability, you can teach your bird to put different-colored rings on the peg in whatever order you choose.

If you want, use the colors of the flag: red, white, and blue. Teach one color at a time, using red first. Once your bird understands that, add the white ring, and so on.

Use the first or second method to train. Any method that was used can be fun if you allow it to be.

Tunnel Walk

This simple behavior is one that is ideal for smaller birds, though any bird can perform it.

Difficulty Level   Easy
Equipment Needed   Large can, bucket, or any circular container.

	The container should have both ends removed, have no sharp edges, and be thoroughly cleansed. Containers made from cardboard are preferable to metal.
Type of Bird	Any, though it is something that little birds do best.
Training Time	5 to 10 minutes per session, depending on the bird's attention span.
Trick Objective	The bird enters one end of the "tunnel" and walks through the prop to the other end.
Trick Analysis	Allowing time for the bird to get used to the prop, slowly guide him through the can until he is able to go through the entire length. Always figure out a cue beforehand and use that consistently.

Step 1

Place the tube on the table with some special treat nearby, or just cuddle with your bird if he does not want the treat. Move closer each time. It may take a week or more before your bird feels comfortable around the prop.

Reward your bird just for touching or going toward the tunnel in Step 1 of this trick.

Step 2

Place the treat right at the opening of the tube. Allow your bird to explore the container and feel comfortable near it. Sound the clicker and reward your bird each time he goes near the prop.

Step 3

Place the treat slightly inside the tube. Keep the tube from rolling by securing it on either side with a small object,

Always end any session on a positive note.

such as a flat rock. Allow your bird to feel comfortable, and reward him each time he puts his head inside. Click and reward each time he does this.

Step 4

Place treats farther inside so that your bird has to go farther to get the treat. Click and reward.

Step 5

Place the treat at the other end of the tunnel, and your bird should go through the entire length to retrieve it. Click and reward.

Take each session at your bird's pace. This will make it more enjoyable.

By placing a treat just inside the tunnel, you encourage your bird to enter.

Eventually, your bird will walk all the way through the tunnel on cue. Remember to reward and praise him.

Bell Ring

Difficulty Level	Easy
Equipment	Bell or bell ring prop
Type of Bird	Any type of bird
Training Session	5-15 minutes per session
Trick Objective	The bird goes over to the hanging bell and hits the bell with his beak, or the bird goes over to the hanging bell and pulls on a string, or the bird goes over to a bell on the table and picks it up and rings it. He could also put it in your hand after he rings it. Another possible option is the desk bell that you see in hotels; he has to hit the little knob on the top to ring it.
Trick Analysis	Decide how you want to proceed. Choose one variation and stick with it. Keep in mind each of the little baby steps needed to perform this behavior.

When you have it clear in your mind how you want to proceed, do so. Think of a cue to use, either verbal or hand cue (or both), and use it from the beginning.

Variation 1

Step 1

Place the prop on the table and allow the bird to get used to it. Reward him just for going near it. Don't rush your bird; let him take his time.

Each time he does go near it or allows you to move it closer to him, sound your clicker and reward him.

Once he is comfortable with the prop near him, you can go on to step 2. Remember, all birds learn at a different rate, some slower, some faster.

Step 2

Now that your bird has accepted the prop, demonstrate the bell. Play with it yourself to get his interest. Some birds will run right over to see what it is you're doing, and they may even hit the bell themselves. If your bird does, sound the clicker and give him the reward immediately.

If he just goes near the bell or touches it, do the same thing. Some birds may need to be lured over to the bell by the use of the treat. Show your bird the treat and entice him over to the bell, putting the treat close to the bell and a little behind it. This forces him to touch the bell in order to get the treat. Sound that clicker and reward him.

Do this until he is comfortable and is starting to touch the bell immediately when you give the cue. If he accomplishes this, move on to step 3.

Step 3

When he touches the bell the next time, hold off on giving him his treat. Hopefully he will hit the bell again, ringing it (however slightly). Sound the clicker and give him his reward.

Keep repeating this step until you get at least one ring each time. Once he is doing this, you can then wait, and with luck, he will ring the bell again.

Click and reward for two rings. Once he is doing this, go on to the final step.

Step 4

When he is ringing the bell two or more times consistently, move the prop away from him slightly, an inch or two each time. When he hits the bell, making it ring each time, you can move it again.

Keep working at this until he goes the distance that you want. Remember that no two birds learn at the same rate. If he seems confused or overly frustrated, back up a step or two and do something that he knows.

Variation 2

Pulling the String From Bell Ring Prop

Train this the same way as the previous variation; however, instead of hitting the bell, the bird will take a string in his beak and pull on it. For this type of prop, you can find a bell or chimes in a craft store. Before you buy, make sure that the material is something that won't harm your bird.

Attach a large bead to a sturdy string and tie so it will sound the chimes

One variation on the bell ring trick is to have your bird pull a string to ring the bell.

when your bird pulls it. Train this by substituting the action of pulling the string for hitting the bell.

Variation 3

Table Bell

You can use any bell that will sit on a table as long as it has a little handle on top, since your bird needs to take hold of something to pick the bell up and ring it. This one can also be considered a retrieval behavior. Start out the same way as you would any behavior.

Let the bird get used to the prop first, then allow him to touch it.

Next, you want to get your bird to pick up the bell, and perhaps ring it. Most likely he will just pick it up, because when he touches it, you're no longer rewarding him.

Once he is holding it, wait a few seconds to see what happens. Most likely, he will do something to make the bell ring. If he does, reward him. After that's accomplished, start to put your hand under the bell. Your bird should ring it and then drop it in your hand. Click and reward.

Once that is occurring reliably, start to move your hand farther away. The final behavior will be to have your bird pick up the bell, ring it, and place it in your hand.

Variation 4

Desk Bell

Once your bird is used to the prop, including its sound, hold the food reward directly over the little knob on top. Let your bird get used to reaching toward that general area first. Once he's comfortable with that, don't let go of the food reward that you're now holding behind the knob. Your bird will have to reach over to get the treat. Because you aren't letting go, your bird

Another variation uses a desk bell. In Step 1, reward your bird when he touches the bell.

might try to pull it from you. When he does this, he will most likely hit that little knob. Sound your clicker and reward him.

Keep doing this until he gets the idea. Soon he will hit the knob first, then ask for his reward. If you want him to hit it more than once, hold off on the clicker and treat. When he does it again, then click and reward.

Bucket Pull

Difficulty Level	Easy
Equipment Needed	T-stand prop with bucket on a chain or rope.
Type of Bird	Any type of bird
Training Session	Sessions can last from 5 minutes to 15 minutes. This simple trick is one that birds enjoy a lot, so sessions may last longer.
Trick Objective	The bird raises the bucket on a chain to get his reward. He could also slide down the rope and remove the treat from the bucket.
Trick Analysis	Figure out your cue first. Using baby steps, gradually lengthen the distance your bird goes to retrieve his reward from the bucket.

Variation 1

Step 1

Put a favorite treat in the bucket that is positioned directly below the T-stand perch. Allow your bird to get used to the prop with the food placed inside. Each time he reaches for the treat, sound your clicker and allow him to take the reward on his own.

Step 2

Lower the bucket about one inch. Allow him to retrieve the treat. Sound the clicker as he gets the reward.

Step 3

Lower the bucket again. Each time you lower the bucket, consider that one training session. Allow your bird to get used to the lower position each time.

Keep replacing his favorite treat into the bucket. Click and reward each time.

Putting a treat inside the bucket will encourage your bird to pull the bucket up to himself. Start training with the bucket close to his perch.

As training continues, gradually lower the bucket until your bird has to pull it up the desired distance. Eventually, you can eliminate placing the treat in the bucket.

Step 4

Lower the bucket again. Keep repeating this step until the bucket is all the way down.

By this step, the bird should no longer be able to just reach down and remove the reward. He will have to figure out how to get the reward on his own. He may use his beak or foot to try to lift the bucket. Click and reward.

You can give him the bucket and allow him to take the reward on his own.

Step 5

He will need to lift the bucket up all the way from the bottom, using either his beak or his foot. Some birds can lift it all the way on one try, while others will lift it slowly, stepping on the excess amount. They will then remove the reward and drop the bucket back down. Some birds may even like a favorite toy in the bucket instead of a treat.

Variation 2

Step 1

This variation is geared more toward smaller birds. Begin with the bucket at a lower level, because your goal is to have your bird slide down the rope. For this variation, it's best to use a cloth rope. Sliding down a chain can be rough on your bird's feet.

Allow the bird to reach down a slight distance to the bucket to retrieve his reward. Millet is the best reward for this trick.

Step 2

Lower the bucket about an inch. Let your bird go down the rope to retrieve his reward. Remember to use the clicker and praise a lot.

Step 3

Slowly lower the rope more each time until it hangs all the way down. Use the clicker, your reward, and lots of praise.

Variation 3

Step 1

Place a ladder nearby; for this trick to work, your bird should already know how to go down it on cue. Leave the bucket all the way down at the bottom. Your bird should go down the ladder. Click and reward him.

Step 2

Entice your bird over to the bucket by showing him the reward. When he goes to the bucket, sound the clicker and reward him.

Step 3

Your bird should go directly to the bucket and looks inside or even gets his own treat.

Step 4

Your bird should go down the ladder, go over to the bucket, and either dump the bucket or go into the bucket to get the treat.

Playing Dead

Difficulty Level	Easy (but requires a lot of trust on your bird's part)
Equipment Needed	None
Type of Bird	Any bird can do this behavior
Training Session	10 minutes per session, or as long as the bird's attention span.
Trick Objective	Getting the bird to lie on his back in your hand or on the table. The bird can also hang upside down on your hand.
Trick Analysis	The bird will start to roll over or allow you to turn him over in your hand. It takes a lot of trust between bird and owner to perform this behavior.

Step 1

Remember to choose a cue. This behavior requires a lot of trust between the trainer and the bird. Not all birds will allow you to do this.

Take one hand and place it on your bird's back, as if you were petting him. (Some birds may bite because they do not like being touched.) If your bird is okay with you doing this, remember to sound the clicker, reward, and praise. Go on to step 2 when your bird allows you to do this readily.

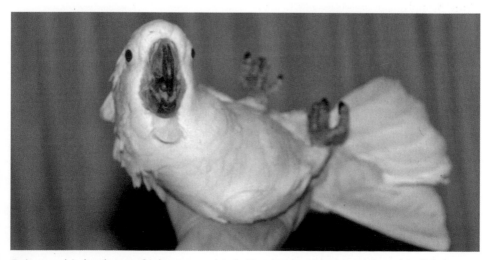

Being on his back may frighten your bird. Go slowly with this trick and build the trust between you and your bird.

If your bird is afraid of being tilted upside down or petted, you may be bitten. Go very slowly and watch your bird for any signs of fright or aggression.

Step 2

Apply very slight pressure and start to tilt your hand slightly. Remember to use the clicker, reward, and praise.

Step 3

This step requires some coordination and trust. Slowly tip your hand over, holding on to the bird's feet in one hand while you are holding him in the other. When he lets you do this each time, go onto step 4. Someone else may have to sound the clicker and give the reward for you. You can still give the praise.

Step 4

When your bird is upside down in your hand, slowly inch your fingers from his feet, which have been holding onto your hand. You may only be able to do one foot at a time. When he is comfortable with this, he will let go easily. Give lots of praise if he does.

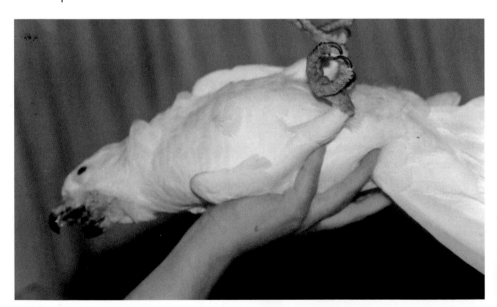

The end result of this trick is your bird lying limp in your hands with his feet in the air. This trick can take quite some time to train, so be patient.

Alternative Method

Some birds find it very natural to be tilted while on the owner's hand and will hang upside down. If your bird does this, place your hand on his back. When he is comfortable with that, place your hand on his back and tilt him so he is on his back. When this occurs easily, you can then remove your fingers until he is lying on your hand.

You can also cradle your bird in your arm like a baby using this same method. (Try giving him a baby bottle to hold while doing this, and rock him like a baby.)

Firefighter

Difficulty Level	Easy
Equipment Needed	Fire engine (best if it is remote controlled)
Type of Bird	Works best with smaller birds, but if you can find a larger engine, then larger birds can ride. Macaw-sized birds might tip the engine over if they try to climb the ladder.
Training Session	10-20 minutes. However, if your bird enjoys riding around on the engine, you can extend the session.
Trick Objective	To get the bird to ride around on the fire engine and walk up the ladder.
Trick Analysis	The bird can be put onto the engine, or else he can walk over to the engine himself and climb on. He will then allow the trainer to move the engine by remote control. When the ladder goes up, the bird will go over to the ladder and climb up to the top. Once on the top, he will play with the hose, making it look like he is helping put out a fire.

Step 1

Decide on a cue. The first step is always to make sure your bird is comfortable around the prop. When your bird is used to the truck, move on to step 2.

In the completed trick, your bird will ride the fire truck and then climb up the ladder.

Step 2

Put your bird on the prop, sound the clicker, and reward. Stretch out the time he has to sit on the prop before he gets the reward. When he is sitting on it for the desired time, go to step 3.

Step 3

Move the prop very slowly, praising your bird as you do so. Each time he allows you to move it, sound the clicker, reward, and praise. When he allows you to move the truck for the desired distance, go on to step 4.

Step 4

Now that the bird is comfortable with the prop moving, you can start either by moving it by remote or by turning it on. Remember to carefully gauge your bird's reaction. Stand by to prevent any accidents, and offer praise continually. Sound the clicker and reward. When he sits on the fire engine without trying to fly off, go on to step 5.

Step 5

The ladder portion of this trick is trained the same way as the ladder behavior discussed previously. Refer to that section for details.

I have trained this behavior so that my cockatiels all come riding in on the fire engine, the ladder goes up, and one by one they all walk up the ladder to the table to get their reward.

Train

Difficulty Level	Easy
Equipment	Toy train
Type of Bird	Works best with smaller birds. If you can find a larger train, a medium to large bird might be able to fit on it.

Training Sessions	10-15 minutes. Some birds really love to ride around on the train, and for these birds, the sessions can be longer.
Training Objective	Having the bird ride on the train.
Trick Analysis	The bird will sit on top of the train while it rides around.

The hardest part of this trick may be finding a train that doesn't go too fast. Stay alert to make sure that your bird does not fall off the prop.

You can set up an entire railroad scene and have your bird ride through villages and towns on the train.

Step 1

Decide on a cue to use for this trick. Allow the bird to get used to the prop while it is stationary; when he does, move on to step 2

Step 2

Get the bird used to the moving train. Move it by hand at first or set it for the slowest speed. Make sure your bird is comfortable and safe. Click, reward, and praise each time he goes near the train.

Step 3

Put the bird on the stationary prop, sound the clicker, and reward. Do not move the prop yet. When he is comfortable on the prop, move on to step 4.

Step 4

With your bird on the train, move it by hand, allowing him to become accustomed to the motion. Clicker, reward, and praise. When your bird is ready, go on to step 5.

Some trains have whistles that may or may not scare your bird. Other trains may puff smoke. If you have a train that does, turn off the smoke feature. The smoke may burn or otherwise harm your bird.

Step 5

Allow the train to move on its own, making sure you are nearby in case the bird is frightened. Some birds will enjoy riding around, while others will try to fly away. If your bird tries to fly away, he may need to go back a step.

Slide

Difficulty Level	Easy to intermediate
Equipment Needed	Slide sized to your bird's needs.
Type of Bird	Any, but the slide must be the right size for the bird.
Training Time	Five to 15 minutes. Some birds really enjoy this behavior, and for them, you can extend the sessions.
Trick Objective	Getting the bird to go down the slide. You can train bigger birds to go up a ladder first.
Trick Analysis	Bird will go up the ladder and then slide down the slide.

This prop can be bought at any toy store. Though it is sized for larger birds, small birds can also be trained to go down the slide. If you have a very small bird, you might want to check out the doll furniture section of a toy store for a smaller version.

It is best not to use a slide that is too slick or steep. If it is too slick or too steep, the bird can slide too fast and end up hurting himself or being frightened, which should never happen during training.

Step 1

Figure out a cue and use that each time. Once again, the idea is to get the bird used to the prop. Once he is comfortable around the prop, go to step 2.

Step 2

If the slide can be flattened so the bird does not slide down it yet, make it flat. Otherwise, you will need to raise the bottom of the slide to make it more level. Place the bird on the level slide. Allow the bird to walk and become

In the first step, your bird gets used to the slide. Elevate the bottom so the slide is more or less level.

As the bird becomes more accustomed to the slide, gradually lower the bottom so that he slides down.

comfortable on the slide. Clicker, reward, and praise the bird. Go on to step 3 when the bird feels comfortable.

Step 3

Raise the slide very slightly, but not enough so the bird slides down it. Put the bird on the slide. If he seems frightened at this point, go back a step. Otherwise, clicker, reward, and praise. When he is comfortable, raise the slide once again.

Step 4

Now that you've raised the slide again, allow enough incline for the bird to slide down. Do not make it so steep that the bird slides down too fast, but do make it steep enough that he can slide down easily. Put the bird on the slide and offer encouragement, enticing him to slide down. If he gets scared, go back a step or decrease the incline.

Step 5

If your bird is enjoying going down the slide, you may also have him walk up the stairs to get to the slide. Place a treat on the stairs.

When he reaches for the treat, sound the clicker, reward, and praise. Once he is doing this, go to step 6.

Step 6

Put the treat up a step or two so that in order to get the treat, the bird has to step up on the ladder. Keep increasing the number of steps he has to go up until he steps up onto the slide. Sound the clicker and reward.

Step 7

Completion of the entire behavior. The bird goes over to the ladder, goes up the ladder, steps up on the slide, and then goes down the slide.

Chapter 5

Intermediate Tricks

Mailbox

Difficulty Level	Intermediate
Equipment Needed	Toy mailbox and letters. These can be bought at any toy store.
Type of Bird	Medium to large birds
Training Sessions	15 minutes per session
Trick Objective	To take the letters out of the mailbox or to put them in.
Trick Analysis	The bird will go over to the mailbox, open it up, and remove letters. He will either place or throw the letters in your hand, or place the letters into the mailbox.

This behavior can be trained in several ways. The bird can also be trained to mail the letters instead of getting them out of the mailbox.

For smaller birds, you can make small letters for them to mail.

Step 1 is to allow your bird to get used to and touch the prop. Placing a treat on the door will help.

Step 1

Place a treat on the door of the mailbox. When the bird goes over to get the treat, as soon as he touches the seed, sound the clicker. As soon as he does this easily, go to step 2.

Step 2

Hold off on the treat. When he touches the mailbox door, sound the clicker. When he does this easily, go to step 3.

Step 3

Now that he is touching the door without hesitation, wait to give him the treat. Eventually, he should grab hold of it. When he does this, sound the clicker. When he grabs it every time, go to step 4.

Step 4

Wait on giving him the treat. Soon he will become frustrated enough to grab hold of the door harder and maybe open it. You can aid in this by making sure the door is slightly ajar. When he does this repeatedly, go on to step 5.

In Step 7, reward your bird when he pulls the letters out of the mailbox. Hold your hand next to the box if you want him to give them to you.

Step 5

The letters should be inside the mailbox. Place a treat on them before starting. When your bird reaches for the treat, sound the clicker and reward him. When he does this easily, go to step 6.

Step 6

Don't give him a treat when he touches the letters. Wait until he grabs hold of one of the letters before sounding the clicker and rewarding him. When he grabs it each time, go on to step 7.

Step 7

Wait until he grabs hold of the letter, but don't do anything. Wait for him to either pull it out or throw it out. If you want him to put it in your hand, make sure your hand is right there. If you want to train him to put it in your hand, go on to step 8 once he is completing this step easily.

Step 8

Move your hand slightly away. With each step, move it away farther, until he has to walk over to drop the letter into your hand.

Answering the Phone

Difficulty Level	Intermediate
Equipment Needed	Toy phone
Type of Bird	Any, but you must gear the prop and training to the bird.
Training Session	10-15 minutes per session
Trick Objective	The bird picks up the phone in his beak or in his foot. For an extra touch, he can bring his beak to the mouthpiece as if he is going to talk into the phone.
Trick Analysis	The bird goes over to the phone, lifts the receiver off the hook with his beak or his foot, and then brings the phone up to his beak. If it is in his beak, he can put it down on the table and then move his beak down to the mouthpiece and talk into it.

Step 1

Place the phone near the bird. Allow the bird to become used to the phone. Sound the clicker, reward, and praise. When the bird is used to the prop, go on to step 2.

At first, you may have to put a treat under the phone receiver to get your bird to touch it.

Step 2

Place a treat under the phone. When the bird touches the phone or moves the handle to get the treat, sound the clicker, reward, and praise. When he does this consistently, go on to step 3.

Step 3

Do not put the treat under the phone handle; instead, wait until your bird either touches the phone handle on his own or actually picks it up with his beak. When he does, sound the clicker, reward, and praise. Stretch out the time that he holds onto the phone. When he does this regularly, go on to step 4.

Step 4

Now that he is picking the phone up, he needs to bring it up closer to his beak. You can get him to do this by smearing a little bit of peanut butter on the mouthpiece. Use very little, just enough so that he gets a lick or two. When he does this consistently, go on to step 5.

If your bird talks, you can also train him to say hello when he answers the phone.

Step 5

Stop using the peanut butter; instead, wait for him to move the mouthpiece closer to his beak. When he does, sound the clicker, reward, and praise. Stretch out the time that he does this. Sound the clicker, reward, and praise.

Playing the Keyboard or Piano

Difficulty Level	Intermediate
Equipment Needed	Keyboard or piano
Type of Bird	Any, but it must be geared to the bird's size. Smaller birds would have a hard time with this because they do not have the strength or weight to hit the keys.
Training Session	5-15 minutes per session
Trick Objective	To get the bird to hit the keys or to walk on them.
Trick Analysis	The bird will go over to the keyboard or the

piano. He will hit the keys with his beak several times in a row, playing a tune The bird can also be taught to play a very simple tune. To do this, start with one key, then the next key that you want him to hit, and so on. This is a chaining behavior. Once he has one key down, add more.

Step 1

Pick that all-important cue first. By offering treats and praise, allow the bird to become used to the prop. When the bird starts going over to the prop consistently, go on to step 2.

Step 2

Place a treat on one of the keys. (If you want the bird to play a very short and simple tune, put the treat on the same starting key each time.) When he pushes the key or just touches the key to get the treat, sound the clicker, reward, and praise. When he does this each time, go on to step 3.

Step 3

Do not put the treat on the key; wait for him to hit it on his own. When he does, sound the clicker, reward, and praise. When he does this each time, go on to step 4.

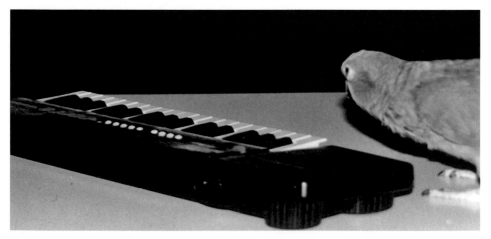

Start training this trick by putting a treat on a key. After your bird is used to that, reward him only when he touches the key on his own.

You can use the clicker and reward system to train your bird to play a short melody.

Step 4

Playing one note is okay; playing many notes or a song is much better. Wait until your bird plays one note, then place a treat on another key. When he goes to get that, sound the clicker, reward, and praise. Once he is playing two notes on a regular basis, you can keep increasing the number of notes he plays. Do not add too many, because your bird will lose interest.

> There are all kinds of pianos that you can get for your bird. They sell a wide variety of them at toy stores. I use an electronic keyboard that sounds a note with only a slight touch.

Banking

Difficulty Level	Intermediate
Equipment Needed	Piggy bank or any other kind of coin bank
Type of Bird	Any size bird, but you need to fit the size of the piggy bank to the bird size.
Training Session	10-20 minutes per session. However, if your bird enjoys the training session, you can extend it.
Trick Objective	To get the bird to put coins in the bank.
Trick Analysis	The bird either picks up a coin on the table

or takes a coin the trainer hands to him and then goes over to the bank and drops the coin inside.

Special Setup

On top of the piggy bank, cut out a larger hole, one where the coin will easily fall through. You can either keep it that size or you can keep replacing the piggy bank and making the hole smaller and smaller each time. It can be very difficult for the bird to get the coin into the small slot.

Step 1

Once you have decided upon a cue, allow the bird to get used to the bank and the coin. When this happens, move on to step 2.

Step 2

With the bank near the bird, hand the bird the coin. If he touches it, sound the clicker, reward, and offer praise. Keep doing this until he is holding onto the coin for a longer period of time. Now go on to step 3.

Step 3

Keeping the coin right over the hole in the piggy bank, let the bird take the coin and then sound the clicker, reward and praise. After a few repetitions, wait to see whether the bird will drop the coin. If he does, sound the clicker, reward, and praise. Keep doing this until he drops it inside the bank every time.

Money can be very dirty, having passed through countless hands. Wash the coins you will be using in this trick before your bird puts them in his mouth.

Step 4

Hand the bird the coin directly over the piggy bank. Click, reward, and praise each time he gets it right. Then start moving the coin farther away. When he is taking the coin from a distance you have decided upon, go to step 5.

Step 5

Now that your bird is taking the coin and putting it in the bank, he can now walk a few steps over to the bank to put the money in. Start with the coin in the position your bird is used to, then move it very slightly. With each progressive step, sound the clicker, reward, then praise. If he feels frustrated at any time, move one step back to something he knows.

At this point, you can decide whether you want to make the hole smaller. If you do, then go to step 6.

Step 6

Decrease the size of the hole very slightly; you still want it to be very easy for your bird to put the coin in. Remember, only reward when the coin goes inside the bank, not when it falls outside the bank. Each time you decrease the size, keep working the behavior until the bird is doing it easily. Then you can decrease the size once again. Keep doing this until it is at the size you want it to be. Remember that the behavior becomes much more difficult the smaller the hole becomes.

Alternative Method: "Toilet" Bank

This bank can be used in several ways. You can train your bird to flush the toilet. If you have the lid up, you can train him to put the lid down, then flush the toilet. You can also have smaller birds sit on the toilet, then get off and flush it. You can even have the bird carry a small newspaper/magazine/book, jump up on the toilet, hold the newspaper with one foot and pretend to read it, then get off and flush.

Basketball

Difficulty Level	Intermediate to Advanced
Equipment Needed	Basketball hoop prop and small wiffle ball.
Type of Bird	Any type of bird who can lift the ball.
Training Time	Varies between birds. This should not be the first behavior that you teach. This one should be taught once your bird has become more familiar with the training game.
Training Objective	The bird will take the ball, walk over to the prop, and drop the ball through the hoop.
Trick Analysis	You need to have this behavior broken

down into little steps before you start to train. Keep your goals in mind prior to training, and have your verbal and/or hand cues ready before you start. It might be easier to train this behavior backwards, starting with the ball partially in the hoop first.

Step 1

Introduce the prop. During the first day or so, let your bird become familiar with the basketball prop and the ball.

Step 2

Place the ball directly over the basketball hoop, slightly inside it. The bird should be able to just touch the ball. Tap it with your finger or use a treat to entice your bird over to the ball.

When he reaches for it or slightly touches it, let the ball go, so that it drops

through the hoop. Sound your clicker and reward the bird. Repeat. When he does this each time, move on to step 3.

Step 3

Lift the ball higher up so that it is just barely out of the basketball hoop. Allow the bird to touch the ball again and then sound the clicker, rewarding him. When he does this consistently, move to the next step.

Step 4

Next time he reaches for the ball, hold off on giving him the treat. Out of frustration, he should try to hold onto the ball longer, rather than just barely touching it.

Allow your bird to get used to the hoop and the ball before moving on to the next step.

When he does this, let the ball go, sound the clicker, and reward him. When he does this several times, move on to the next step.

Step 5

Now that the bird is holding the ball longer, start moving it slightly away from the hoop. By doing this, you are trying to get him to move the ball back to the hoop. He might need some help in the beginning. Sound the clicker and reward the bird.

Step 6

By now, your bird should be holding the ball slightly longer than a mere touch. He should also be moving it slightly toward the hoop.

Now he needs to hold onto the ball longer and to start putting it into the hoop himself. Hold off on the treat and let him take the ball and put it into the hoop. Remember, you have just barely moved the ball from directly over the basketball hoop. It should only be a fraction of an inch.

When he takes the ball and puts it into the hoop, sound the clicker and reward him. If he shows any signs of frustration, back up a step or two. He may not understand what it is that you want yet.

Step 7

As your bird gets better at putting the ball into the basket (actually just

When your bird is holding the ball for longer durations, start moving the ball farther from the hoop.

In Step 6, your bird gets a reward when he puts the ball through the hoop.

Finally, your bird gets the ball, brings it to the hoop, and drops it in.

dropping the ball into the basket), start moving it farther away from him. Do not move it too far, because that will frustrate him. At each new distance, sound the clicker and reward him.

Step 8

Eventually you will get to the point where you can move the ball far away from the hoop and your bird will walk over to get the ball and then walk to the hoop and slam dunk it.

Chapter 6

Advanced Tricks

Ball Walk

Difficulty Level	Advanced, mainly due to the balancing necessary.
Equipment needed	Ball geared to bird's size. Tracks optional.
Type of Bird	Any, but for smaller birds you will need to move the ball.
Training Time	10 minutes or longer, depending on the bird's attention span.
Trick Objective	Getting the bird to step up onto the ball and walk.
Trick Analysis	The bird steps up on the ball and you move it slightly away from you, causing the bird to walk up the ball, toward you.

Step 1

Figure out a cue and use that each time. The first step is getting your bird used to the ball, which is a major step for many birds. Once your bird is used to the ball, go on to step 2.

Step 2

Place the bird on top of the ball and reward, offering lots of praise. Do not move the ball yet, since birds do not like feeling unbalanced. If the ball is stable, your bird will most likely be willing to step up on it.

This is where a track of some sort is useful. You can put a small block in front of and behind the ball to stop it from rolling. Once your bird steps up on the ball without problems and does not mind sitting there, go on to step 3.

Step 3

You need to be very coordinated or have an extra hand to complete this next step. Slowly roll the ball away from you, which should cause your bird to walk forward and up. Keep a treat in front of your bird to entice him. When he takes his first step, sound the clicker, praise, and reward him. Do this with each step. Once this is happening easily, go to step 4.

Step 4

This step is an extension of step 3; the bird stays on the ball, but takes more than one step. Eventually, the bird should walk up the ball for the entire distance. When the bird does this each time, you may want to go onto step 5.

Step 5

Because of their size, smaller birds may not be able to move the ball without help. Larger birds should have no problems.

By now the bird is used to sitting and walking on the ball. The next step is to have him do this on his own. I have found that it's easier for the bird if you keep the ball inside a track, because he is not fighting with a ball that moves all over the place. I also cheat slightly when first starting to train this; I raise the track on one end very slightly so the ball will roll more easily.

Place the bird on top of the ball. This time, do not move the ball. The bird should have an idea by now that he needs to walk in order to get the treat held out in front of him. As soon as he does, praise, clicker, and reward. When he does this all the time, go on to step 6.

Step 6

Withhold the treat, and don't give it to him once he takes one step. You want him to take more steps. Eventually you want him to walk the entire track on the ball. Reward with each progressive step. For example, if he takes two steps, reward; next time reward for four steps, etc.

Riding a Scooter

Difficulty Level	Advanced
Equipment Needed	Small toy scooter (can be purchased at most toy stores)
Type of Bird	Large birds
Training Session	10-15 minutes per session
Trick Objective	Getting the bird to ride the scooter.
Trick Analysis	The bird will go over to the scooter and get on it. Once on the scooter, the bird will then place his beak on the bar and push it down the table with one foot like a child would ride a scooter.

Scooters are hard to find. Most of the scooters on the market today are made from lightweight material. If you can find one that is made from metal, get that type instead, or try to add more weight to the platform to make it more stable.

Metal scooters are better for this trick than plastic ones because they are more stable.

Step 1

Select a cue. Place the scooter on the table. Allow the bird to become comfortable around the scooter. Once he is, go to step 2.

Step 2

Place the treat near the handle of the scooter. When the bird touches the handle, sound the clicker, reward, and praise. When he easily does this each time, go to step 3.

> Work on a smooth surface. Make sure the scooter is easy to move.

Step 3

This requires some coordination. You need to get the bird standing alongside the scooter, and he needs to touch the handle. Use the treat to get him into the right position, or else move the scooter into the right position. Sound the clicker, reward, and praise each time he gets it right. Then move on to step 4.

Step 4

For this step, your bird needs to hold onto the handle longer while in the right position. He may or may not move the scooter slightly while doing this. Once he does this each time, go to step 5.

Once your bird gets himself positioned correctly, start rewarding him only when he gets the scooter to move.

Step 5

You may need to move the scooter slightly so that your bird steps up on it. You can also manipulate your bird to get him into the right position. Go slowly, use the clicker, reward, and praise, even if the bird moves very slightly. Stretch it out longer each time. When your bird does this consistently, go on to step 6.

Step 6

Hold off on offering the clicker. You may need to move the scooter slightly. When your bird lifts his foot, sound the clicker, reward, and praise. Keep doing this, and when he is doing this on a regular basis, go to step 7.

Step 7

Do not sound the clicker when your bird moves once. Hold off. He may move again. When he does, sound the clicker, reward, and praise. Keep stretching out the time between sounding the clicker, reward, and praise. Eventually he will scoot across the table.

Bowling

Difficulty Level	Advanced
Equipment Needed	Bowling lane, ball, pins
Type of Bird	All species, but the trick must be geared to the bird's size.
Training Session	10-15 minutes per session
Trick Objective	Getting the bird to bowl.
Trick Analysis	The bird will push the bowling ball with his beak and try to get as many pins down as he can.

Step 1

Pick a cue that you want to use. When your bird is comfortable around the prop, go on to step 2.

Step 2

This step involves cheating slightly. Set up the pins, the little stand, and the alley. Place the ball on the little spot that was intended for it. Place a small piece of your

If you let your bird play with the pins and ball at the start of training, he may get used to the prop more quickly.

bird's favorite treat as close to the ball as you can get it. Place the bird on the little stand. When he reaches for the treat, he will actually touch the ball. When he does, sound the clicker and give him the reward and lots of praise. Keep doing this until he does it comfortably. Then go on to step 3.

Step 3

Show your bird the treat and then place it under the ball. When the bird pushes the ball the get the treat, sound the clicker, reward, and praise. When he does this consistently, go on to step 4.

Step 4

This time do not use the treat; hold off on it. When your bird touches the ball, sound the clicker, reward, and offer lots of praise. At first, reward any movement toward the ball. Remember that your bird does not see that treat nearby. When your bird is consistently pushing the ball down the lane, try seeing how many strikes he can get.

In Step 2, place a treat under the ball to encourage your bird to knock the ball down the lane.

Eventually, your bird will be able to repeat this trick and bowl a short game. If you have multiple birds, you can keep score for each and see who wins.

Golfing

Difficulty Level	Advanced
Equipment Needed	Golf ball and golf set (you may have to build it yourself).
Type of Bird	Medium to large
Training Session	10-15 minutes per session
Trick Objective	Getting a hole in one
Trick Analysis	The bird will pull back on the ball that holds the golf club. The ball will then go down the runway and end up as a hole in one.

Step 1

Don't forget to pick a cue. Depending on the prop, you may need to train this in different ways, but your first step should be to get the bird accustomed to the prop.

Step 2

Place your bird on the T-stand. Place a favorite treat inside the little ball that is part of the handle. When he goes for the treat, sound the clicker and

If your bird is a good talker, you can train him to say "Fore" before he pulls on the club handle.

reward and praise. If you use a small club instead, hand the bird the club, and when he touches it with his beak, sound the clicker, reward, and praise.

When the bird is performing either action consistently, you can move on to step 3.

Step 3

With your bird on the stand and the treat inside the ball, hold off on sounding the clicker. Wait until the bird holds onto the ball longer or actually pulls the handle back. If he does either, sound the clicker, reward, and offer praise.

Offer the club to the bird, but this time, instead of rewarding him just for touching it, wait until he holds onto it longer. When he does, sound the clicker, reward, and offer lots of praise.

When the bird performs either action consistently, go on to step 4.

Step 4

This time do not put the treat inside the ball on the handle. Wait for your bird to grab hold of the handle. He may either grab it or actually pull it back. If he does either, sound the clicker, reward, and praise.

Now that your bird is holding onto the club longer, place the ball near the club. If he does not drop the club when the ball is up against it—even if it is for a second or two—sound the clicker, reward, and praise. When he does either consistently, go to step 5.

Step 5

With your bird on the stand, hold off on the treat until he actually pulls it back. At this point, you should put the golf ball in the proper position. If you set up the prop correctly, all it will take is a slight pull on the handle to release the club.

Each time your bird does this, sound the clicker and then reward and offer praise. Keep doing this until your bird is doing this consistently. Try to see how many holes in one your bird can get. (Hint: the better you set it up, the more likely it is that he will get a hole in one.)

With the bird holding onto the golf club and touching the ball with the club, wait until he moves the ball more. When he does, sound the clicker, reward, and praise. Stretch out the time and the distance the bird hits the ball.

Skating

Difficulty Level	Difficult
Equipment Needed	Skates and training bars
Type of Bird	Large birds
Training Sessions	10-15 minutes per session
Trick Objective	Get the bird to roller skate.
Trick Analysis	Get the bird to go up on the skates, using the training bars get him to move his feet straight while pushing the skates. Eventually get rid of the training bars and have him move the skates on his own.

Skating is one of the hardest behaviors to train, and skates can be very hard to find. Because most props today are made with lightweight materials, many of the skates available are too light. Skates do come with training dowels to help teach the bird to move his feet properly.

Step 1

This is one of the most difficult behaviors to train. Parrots walk pigeon-toed, and because of this, they tend to crash the skates into each other. Once you've chosen the cue, start getting your bird used to the prop. When he is comfortable around the prop, go to step 2.

Step 2

You can either have the bird step up on the prop or else you can put him on it. I started by putting my bird Charlie on the prop, making sure I held the skates very steadily. Sound the clicker, reward, and praise. When he is sitting comfortably on the skates without moving them, move on to step 3.

It is very hard for some birds to push the skates. Until they can get the motions down, they may end up doing splits. This is never a good thing. If your bird is having trouble, help him out a little.

Step 3

With the training sticks in place, move one of the skates forward. Sound the clicker, reward, and praise. Repeat this with the other skate. Keep doing this until your bird is comfortable. This teaches your bird to move the skates straight.

This step may take a long time. Be patient. When he is performing several skates in a row, move on to step 4.

Step 4

Now comes the difficult part. Keep the training sticks in place, but instead of moving them for him, make your bird move them for himself. When he

Because birds' feet curve inward, this behavior may be difficult for your pet to master. With patience and encouragement, he'll get it.

does, he may not go straight at first. That is what the sticks are for, since you will need to correct his path. Hold off on giving the reward. If he moves even a fraction of an inch, sound the clicker. Reward and praise. Keep doing this until your bird is moving easily. Then go onto step 5.

Step 5

Remove the training sticks from the skates. By now your bird should be moving the skates on his own. Make sure that he is still going straight; you may need to correct his path every so often.

Stacking Cups

Difficulty Level	Advanced
Equipment Needed	Stacking cups
Type of Bird	Any size bird, but you need to fit the size of the stacking cups to the bird size.
Training Session	10-20 minutes per session. However, if your bird enjoys playing with the cups, then you can extend the session.
Trick Objective	To get the bird to stack the cups in order.
Trick Analysis	The bird puts one cup into another, going from the largest to the smallest. This behavior not only shows off a bird's intelligence but the fact that parrots can see in color.

Step 1

Chose a cue. Start off with the first and largest cup. When your bird is comfortable, go to step 2.

Step 2

Balance the cup that goes inside the first one on top of the first cup. Place a treat inside that cup. When the bird goes to get the treat, sound the clicker, reward, and praise. If you have it balanced correctly, the cup will fall into the other cup. Keep doing this until the bird pushes the cup into the other cup. Then go to step 3.

Step 3

Move the cup to a position where the bird has to manipulate it to get it inside the other cup. This step sometimes goes slowly, and you may have to back it up a step. If your bird does this, keep moving the cup until it is on the table with the other cup and not on it. Then go to step 4.

Step 4

Once your bird is picking up the other cup and placing it inside the larger cup, add a new cup. Each time you add a cup, train it the same way you did in step 2 and 3. Keep doing this until you are out of cups.

Shopping Cart

Difficulty Level	Advanced
Equipment Needed	Shopping cart (can be purchased at most toy stores and even some pet stores)
Type of Bird	Any size bird, but you need to fit the size of the shopping cart to the bird size.
Training Session	10-20 minutes per session. However, if your bird enjoys playing with the shopping cart, you can extend the session.
Trick Objective	To get the bird to push the shopping cart.
Trick Analysis	The bird takes hold of the handle of the shopping cart and pushes it down the table.

Step 1

Figure out a cue, and get the bird comfortable around the prop. When this occurs, go on to step 2.

Step 2

Now that the bird is used to the prop, he needs to take hold of the handle. Depending on the prop, it may have a little groove in the handle or some plastic around it. If it does, you can put a little piece of treat in there. When he goes to reach for the treat, sound the clicker, reward, and offer praise. Keep doing this until the bird is doing this consistently. Then go to step 3.

Step 3

Do not put a treat in the handle; wait for your bird to take hold of it on his own. When he does this, click and reward. Repeat, gradually increasing the amount of time your bird holds onto the handle before getting the reward. When he holds onto it for an amount of time you decide upon, go on to step 4.

Step 4

Your bird is now holding onto the prop. Slowly move the cart. If he lets go, do not reward him, but if he takes a step or just moves his head, sound the clicker, reward, and praise. Keep doing this until he is walking as you move the cart. Then go to step 5.

Step 5

Begin by moving the cart for him, then hold off and wait. If he moves the cart on his own even slightly, sound the clicker, reward, and praise. Keep doing this, holding off on the reward longer and longer until he is pushing the cart all the way down by himself.

Bonus Steps

You can also have him "go shopping" before pushing the cart. Go to the toy store and pick up some toy foods. Have him pick up the "food," or else hand it to him and then have him put it in the cart. Start with the food over the cart.

When he touches the food, let it go so that it drops into the cart. Sound the clicker, reward, and praise. Keep doing this repeatedly, lengthening the amount of time he holds the food. When he takes it from your hand and drops it into the cart, sound the clicker, reward, and praise.

Lower your hand each time he completes a step, and keep repeating this until your hand is resting on the table and he is picking up the "food" from the table and putting it into the cart.

Decide upon the number and types of "food" your bird needs to put into the cart. You can even train him to pick up the "food" along the way and put it into the cart.

Building the Props

Building the Ring Toss Prop

Wooden Version

Equipment needed: Small wooden base
One flange or torque escherion
2-4 screws
PVC or CPVC
Cap
Rings
Screwdriver
Utility knife or sharp tool (to cut tile and piping)

If you're using PVC and flange, you will also need a male adapter.
If you want to make the prop more permanent, use glue, but make sure you wipe the excess away thoroughly.
To make this prop look more finished, you can add self-sticking tile. It also makes cleanups much easier.

Supplies needed for building the ring toss prop.

The complete ring toss prop.

Step 1: Optional

Cut the self-sticking tile to the base size and attach.

Step 2

Attach the flange or torque escherion to the base with the screws.

Step 3

Cut the PVC or CPVC to an appropriate height for your bird. Then push the piping into the flange. (For PVC, add the male adapter first, then add the piping.)

Step 4

Push the cap onto the top of the piping.

Step 5

Add the rings.

All Wooden Version

Equipment Needed   Wooden Base
Self-sticking tile (optional)
Dowel
Sandpaper
All-purpose glue

Drill

Utility knife or sharp tool (to cut tile and trim dowel)

Step 1

Trim tile to size and attach to base.

Step 2

Cut dowel to an appropriate length for your bird. Trim to round off the upper edge and then sand smooth. (Lengths of dowel are inexpensive and are available at home improvement stores.)

Step 3

Drill an approximately centered hole in the base. (If the base is thick enough, you need not go all the way through.) The hole should match the dowel size well enough for the dowel to be securely glued into the base. The dowel width can be trimmed for a snug fit in a slightly smaller hole.

Step 4

Spread glue liberally in the base's hole and insert dowel. Wipe off excess glue and allow it to dry. Now you're ready for your bird's reaction!

Building The Bell Prop

Equipment Needed

Supplies needed for building the bell prop.

PVC
Male adapter
End cap
Elbow
Flange
4 wood screws
S-hook
Eye
Bell, any shape
Base
Pliers
Screwdriver

Saw or pipe cutters
Self-sticking floor tile (optional;
to make the base easy to clean)

Step 1: Optional

Measure the self-sticking floor tile and cut it to the size of the base. Attach.

Step 2

Attach flange to the base with the wood screws.

Step 3

Screw male adapter into the flange.

Step 4

Cut appropriate length of PVC and push into the male adapter. Push elbow into the PVC.

Step 5

Push a small section of PVC into other end of elbow.

Step 6

Drill a small hole into the end of the cap. Screw the eyehook into the PVC.

Step 7

Screw the nut onto the end of the screw inside the end cap.

Step 8

Place end cap on the PVC.

Step 9

Put the S-hook onto the eye, and, using pliers, squeeze the end that is in the eye closed.

Here is the completed bell prop.

Step 10

Place the bell on the S-hook and squeeze it closed with the pliers.

Step 11

Attach the bell to the end of the S-hook and squeeze it shut with pliers.

Building the Bucket Pull Prop T-Stand

Equipment Needed

Base (larger birds need a larger and heavier base, 2 ft. x 2 ft; smaller birds, 1 ft. x 1 ft.)
Flange
Handle
4 wheels
PVC T-connector with inside threads
Metal pipe (between 2-4 ft, depending on size of the chain and bird). Can be bought at your local hardware store. If it doesn't already have threads on it, they can add the threads there.
24 screws
2 PVC end caps
Rope or chain
Bucket

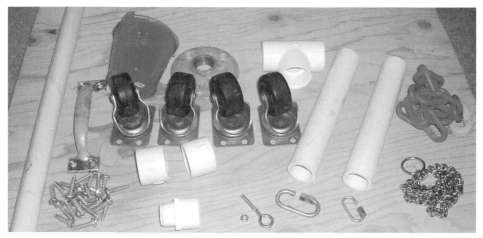

Supplies needed for building the bucket pull prop.

2 rings, such as C-rings or O-rings
Nut
Eye (from the hook and eye)
PVC (cut to the right size to make a perch)
Self-sticking floor tile (optional, for easy cleanup and finished look)
Screwdriver or drill
PVC pipe cutter

Step 1: Optional

Measure base and cut the self-sticking floor tile to size and attach.

Step 2

Screw each of the wheels into the corners of the base.

Step 3

Screw the handle in between two of the wheels.

Step 4

Flip the base over. Attach the flange to the base using four screws.

Step 5

Drill a hole into one of the end caps.

You can use a food cup instead of a bucket. Use a bolt and eye to attach the cup to the chain.

Step 10: Screw the perch onto the metal pole.

Step 6

Screw the eye into the end cap.

Step 7

Attach a nut to the eye inside the end cap.

Step 8

Attach the two PVC pipes into the T-connector.

Step 9

Push the two end caps on each end of the PVC.

Step 10

Screw the metal pipe into the flange.

Step 11

Screw the T-connector into the metal pipe.

Step 12

Attach C-ring to the eye.

Step 13

Attach the chain to the C-ring.

Step 14: Attach the c-ring to the chain.

Step 15: Attach the bucket to the c-ring

Step 14

Attach the C-ring to the other end of the chain.

Step 15

Attach the bucket to the C-ring.

Helpful Hint

This prop also doubles as a stand. It is easy to move because of the wheels and is easy to take apart and carry because of the handle. PVC is very strong and can withstand even the biggest birdie beaks.

Make sure everything fits tightly and is secure.

If you can't find a bucket, use a bird plastic or metal food cup. Drill a hole and attach another eye and nut to it.

Building the Basketball Prop

Wooden Version

Equipment Needed

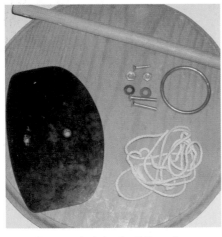

Supplies needed for building the basketball prop.

Wooden base
Wooden dowel
Screws
Metal ring
Washer
Nuts
Plexiglas or acrylic for backboard
String
Drill with wood boring bit
Screwdriver
Circular saw or saber saw
Sandpaper or electric sander
Vise

Step 1: Optional

If you want a fancy-looking basketball court, add a self-sticking wood-grain tile to the base.

Step 2

Using the wood boring drill bit, drill a hole into the base. Do not drill all the way through.

Step 3

With a drill bit, drill a small hole into the end of the wooden dowel.

Step 4

Drill two holes into the wooden dowel near the top.

Step 5

Drill two holes into the Plexiglas near the center.

Step 6

Clamp the metal ring in a vise. With a metal drill bit, drill a small hole into the ring.

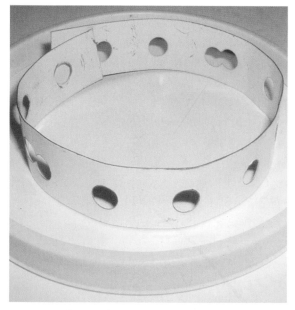

You can choose from a variety of hoops.

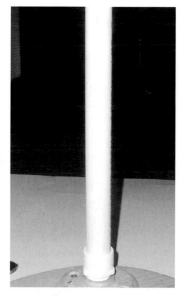

Step 4: Push the pole into the male adapter.

Step 7

Fit the wooden dowel into the hole in the base, with the hole in the wooden dowel facing downward. With a screw, fasten to the base.

Step 8

Attach the Plexiglas backboard to the wooden dowel with one screw and one washer.

Step 9

You can add the string to the hoop at this point. Then, using one screw and one washer, screw the ring into the other hole in the backboard.

Step 10

Secure the hoop and backboard to the wooden dowel using the two nuts.

Finish

Now all you need is a small Wiffle ball and you're set to go.

Wood and PVC Version

Equipment Needed Wooden base
Flange
Screws (for the flange)
PVC cut to your bird's height
Male adaptor
Plexiglas or acrylic backboard
Cap
Wood ring
Metal
Hose clamp that has the clamp piece removed or a roll of punch-holed metal strip
Screws (for the backboard and the hoop)
Tile for the base (optional)
Lightweight ball (such as a Wiffle ball)
Drill

Screwdriver
Sandpaper
Electric saw or saber saw
For fancier baskets, string can be tied
together for the basketball net

Step 1

With the four screws, attach the flange to the base.

Step 2

Screw the male adapter into the flange.

Step 3

Drill holes into the PVC.

Step 4

Push the PVC pipe into the male adapter.

Step 5

Push an end cap onto one end of the PVC pipe.

Step 6

Drill a hole into the Plexiglas.

Step 7

Drill a hole into the hoop.

Step 8

Attach the backboard and hoop to the PVC with one screw.

This is the wooden version of the basketball prop. Remember to size all the props for your bird.

Optional

Add string to make the basketball net. You may find that some species of birds will be more interested in the string than in the prop. For this reason, you may not want to use the string.

Building the Bowling Prop

Equipment Needed   Saw
Drill
Wood glue
Super glue
4 wood screws
Flange
Male adapter
T-connecter
Wood ball (or golf ball)
Bowling pins
PVC piping (sized for your bird)
One piece of wood (for the lane), a minimum of 16" x 2.5" x 0.5".
One piece of wood (sides of lanes) a minimum of 30" x 1.75" x .25" each.
One piece of wood a minimum of 10" x 1" x 1"

Optional materials include 2 end caps, small nails, and small screws.

1 inch=2.54 centimeters
1 cm=10 millimeters
10 millimeters=0.3937 inches

You will also need a piece of wood from which you can cut one to two pieces, each around 5.5 x 5.5 x 0.75 inches for the main base and pin base (for small size birds). You also will need to cut this piece of wood 5.5 x 5.5 x 0.75 inches for the other pin base regardless of bird size. If you have a medium or large bird, then you also will need to have a piece of wood either 8.5 x 8.5 x 0.75 inches (for medium size birds) or 11 (or 12) x 11 (or 12) x 0.75 inches.

You can buy the bowling pins at a toy store or a bakery supply store.

Step 1

For the bases, cut one base around 5.5 x 5.5 x 0.75. This is ideal for small sized birds. Cut the other base around the same size. For medium and large birds, cut one base around the above size and the other base to either 8.5 x 8.5 x 0.75 or 11 or 12 x 12 x 0.75 depending on the size of the bird.

Step 2

For the lane, cut one piece of wood around 15 x 2.5 x 0.5 inches.

Step 3

For the sides of the lane, cut the 0.25 inch wood into 2 pieces each around 15 x 1.75 x 0.25 inches.

Step 4

For the legs cut five pieces of wood from the 1inch wood to around 2 x 1 x 1 each.

Step 5

Cut one piece of wood around 2.5 x 0.5 x 0.5 inches. (If you bought exactly the size of wood you need this will be the only piece left over.)

Step 6

Cut two pieces of acrylic around 5.5 x 5.5 inches.

I find it best to buy more wood than you need. This allows for mistakes made when measuring and cutting. Any wood left over can be used to build more props.

Step 7

Cut one of the pieces of acrylic at a diagonal so you end up with two triangles.

Step 8

Attach the flange to the one of the main base with the four wood screws. (Drill small holes first to make this easier.)

Step 9

With the wood glue, carefully attach each of the four legs to the other side (bottom) of the base from where the flange is. Let dry around 30 minutes. (If you are very talented you can drill holes into the base countersinking them and then attach the legs with screws.)

Step 10

Cut out a piece of PVC around 1-2 inches in height. You may need to make adjustments to fit your bird.

Step 11

Attach the T-connecter to the PVC pipe.

Step 12

Cut out two pieces of PVC for the perch. Judge what your bird will feel most comfortable with.

Step 13

You can add the end caps if you want to at this point.

Step 14

Taking the wood used for the lane attach one side of the side pieces with wood glue, wait around 30 minutes before attaching the other side. You can use small little tack nails to hold this in place better. Make sure that you wipe off any extra glue.

Step 15

Decide which end you are going to use as the front and which the end for the lane. Then attach the fifth leg to the bottom side of the front end of the lane.

Step 16

Attach the small 2 x 0.5 x 0.5 inch piece of wood to the other end of the lane.

Step 17

Using super glue, attach the acrylic to the other base. Wait until it dries before attaching the triangle pieces to either side. Wipe up any extra glue.

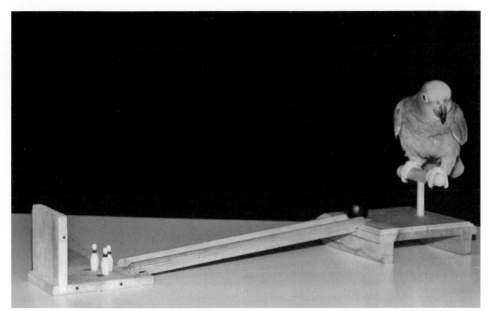

Here is the completed bowling prop.

Step 18

If you are more skilled you can drill small holes in the acrylic and add small screws to secure it.

Step 19

You can also attach the legs on the lane using small screws, but you have to make sure that the screws are flush with the wood.

Step 20

Line up the lane with the main base and then line up on the other end the pin base. Make any adjustments to height if needed. Add pins on the pin base. Add the ball to the small space between the lane and main base.

Resources

ORGANIZATIONS

American Federation of Aviculture
P.O. Box 7312
N. Kansas City, MO 64116
Telephone: (816) 421-2473
E-mail: afaoffice@aol.com
www.afa.birds.org/

Avicultural Society of America
P.O. Box 5516
Riverside, CA 92517-5516
Telephone: (909) 780-4102
E-mail: info@asabirds.org
www.asabirds.org/index.php

Aviculture Society of the United
Kingdom
Arcadia-The Mounts-East Allington-
Totnes
Devon TQ9 7QJ
United Kingdom
E-mail: admin@avisoc.co.uk
www.avisoc.co.uk/

British Bird Council
1st Floor Offices
1159 Bristol Road South
Northfield, Birmingham, B31 2SL
Telephone: 44 01214-765999
www.britishbirdcouncil.com/

The Parrot Society of Australia
P.O. Box 75
Salisbury, Queensland 4107
Australia
E-mail: petbird@parrotsociety.org.au
www.parrotsociety.org.au

PUBLICATIONS

Bird Talk Magazine
3 Burroughs
Irvine, CA 92618
Telephone: (949) 855-8822
Fax: (949) 855-3045
www.animalnetwork.com/birdtalk/d
efault.asp

Bird Times Magazine
7-L Dundas Circle
Greensboro, NC 27407
Telephone: (336) 292-4047
E-mail: info@petpublishing.com
www.petpublishing.com/birdtimes/

Pet & Aviary Birds Magazine
P.O. Box 30806
Knoxville, TN 37930-0806
Telephone: (800) 487-3333
Fax: (865) 690-4941
www.petandaviarybirds.com/

INTERNET RESOURCES

The Parrot Pages
(www.parrotpages.com)
This website includes links to many
different bird organizations, online
magazines, veterinary organizations,
species information, and bird-related
upcoming events.

BirdCLICK
(www.geocities.com/Heartland/
Acres/9154/)
A site and e-mail list devoted to
clicker training pet birds.

Karen Pryor's Clickertraining.com
(www.clickertraining.com)
One of the pioneers of clicker training,
Pryor's website has a wealth of
information on everything from the
principles of positive reinforcement to
upcoming events in the world of
clickers.

UK Clicker Training
(www.clickeruk.com)
British clicker trainer Kay Laurence's
approach focuses on dogs but can be
applied to any animal.

The Parrot Society of Australia
(www.parrotsociety.org.au)
A non-profit organization dedicated
to the promotion and dissemination
of information on the breeding,
keeping, care and conservation of all
parrot species.

VETERINARY RESOURCES
Association of Avian Veterinarians
P.O. Box 811720
Boca Raton, FL 33481-1720
Telephone: (561) 393-8901
E-mail: AAVCTRLOFC@aol.com
www.aav.org/

EMERGENCY RESOURCES AND RESCUE ORGANIZATIONS
ASPCA Animal Poison Control Center
Telephone: (888) 426-4435
E-mail: napcc@aspca.org (for non-
emergency, general information only)
www.apcc.aspca.org

Bird Hotline
P.O. Box 1411
Sedona, AZ 86339-1411
E-mail: birdhotline@birdhotline.com
www.birdhotline.com/

Feathered Friends Adoption and
Rescue
222 S.W. Dillon Ct.
Port St. Lucie, FL 34953-6203
Telephone: (772) 343-8935
E-mail: jesbirds@msn.com
hometown.aol.com/MAHorton/FFAP.
html

RSPCA
Wilberforce Way
Southwater
Horsham, West Sussex RH13 9RS
Telephone: 0870 3335 999
www.rspca.org.uk

RSPCA Australia
P.O. Box 265
Deakin West ACT 2600
Telephone: 02 6283 8300
www.rspca.org.au

Index

Photos

Larry Allan: 7, 12, 13, 15, 17, 24, 26, 27, 28, 55

Isabelle Francais: 22

Leslie Leddo: 6

All other photos by Robin Deutsch